STUDENT RESOURCE WORKBOOK

for

PUBLIC SPEAKING: A CULTURAL PERSPECTIVE

CLELLA JAFFE, Ph.D.

St. John's University, New York

Wadsworth Publishing Company

I(T)P™ An International Thomson Publishing Company

Belmont • Albany • Bonn • Boston • Cincinnati • Detroit • London • Madrid • Melbourne
Mexico City • New York • Paris • San Francisco • Singapore • Tokyo • Toronto • Washington

COPYRIGHT © 1995 by Wadsworth Publishing Company
A Division of International Thomson Publishing Inc.
I(T)P The ITP logo is a trademark under license.

Printed in the United States of America
1 2 3 4 5 6 7 8 9 10—01 00 99 98 97 96 95

For more information, contact Wadsworth Publishing Company.

Wadsworth Publishing Company
10 Davis Drive
Belmont, California 94002, USA

International Thomson Publishing Europe
Berkshire House 168-173
High Holborn
London, WC1V 7AA, England

Thomas Nelson Australia
102 Dodds Street
South Melbourne 3205
Victoria, Australia

Nelson Canada
1120 Birchmount Road
Scarborough, Ontario
Canada M1K 5G4

International Thomson Editores
Campos Eliseos 385, Piso 7
Col. Polanco
11560 México D.F. México

International Thomson Publishing GmbH
Königswinterer Strasse 418
53227 Bonn, Germany

International Thomson Publishing Asia
221 Henderson Road
#05-10 Henderson Building
Singapore 0315

International Thomson Publishing Japan
Hirakawacho Kyowa Building, 3F
2-2-1 Hirakawacho
Chiyoda-ku, Tokyo 102, Japan

Printer: Malloy Lithographing, Inc.

ISBN 0-534-23065-2

Contents

━━━━━

UNIT III   APPLIED CONTEXTS   **95**

Preface

Welcome to public speaking, one of the oldest academic disciplines in the Western university curriculum. Rhetoric, or public speaking, as a subject dates back at least 2500 years.

The purpose of this course is to introduce you to some of the most common forms of public speaking in the United States. Knowing how to organize your ideas and present them publicly will empower you in a culture that values communication skills in the workplace. In addition, you will learn about other speaking traditions—both those from co-cultural groups within the United States and those from global cultures. This is important in a world that is increasingly becoming smaller as media, immigration, international trade, and other factors bring people from different cultural traditions face-to-face in communication events.

This course balances principle and practice. Your textbook presents theories, concepts, and terminology. This Student Resource Workbook contains worksheets and assignments that will guide you as you put theory into practice. There is not enough time in a single academic term to give every type of speech described here and in the text; however, these guidelines may be useful in your future speaking. Each assignment describes a type of speech and is followed by an evaluation form. Your instructor may want to use these forms in assessing your grade; alternatively, you may use them as guides or checklists as you prepare your speech.

Course Objectives

- Given a purposive public speaking situation, you will be able to prepare and deliver a speech appropriate to that situation.
- Given a purposive speaking presentation, you will be able to listen to the speeches of others and evaluate their presentations using criteria developed in the course.
- Your understanding of both Western traditions and other speaking and listening traditions will increase, making you a more effective participant in an increasingly pluralistic culture and shrinking world.

Instructor: _____

Office Location: _____ Office Hours: _____

Campus Phone Number: _____

Rhetoric, I shall argue, should be a study of misunderstanding and its remedies. We struggle all our days with misunderstandings and no apology is required for any study which can prevent or remove them.

I. A. Richards, *Philosophy of Rhetoric*

UNIT I

Principles of Speaking and Listening

Introduction to Public Speaking

COURSE REQUIREMENTS

Quintilian, a first century A.D. Roman educator, provided a detailed account of the ideal education of a public speaker. He emphasized four areas of competency necessary for a good speaker: reading, writing, listening, and speaking. These four areas serve as the focus for the requirements of most public speaking courses. In addition, the Roman phrase, *Vir bonum dicendi peritus* (the good person, skilled in speaking) stresses the importance of ethics in public speaking.

The Reading Requirements

In addition to the text, *Public Speaking: A Cultural Perspective* by Clella Jaffe, you will read supplementary sources as you research your speech topics and find supporting materials for your speeches. Using a variety of sources with different perspectives will help you better understand your topics. Consider reading a major newspaper, such as the *New York Times* or *The Washington Post*, regularly during this quarter.

For example: Julie Graef read articles from the *New York Times*, *Jet*, *Ebony*, *Newsweek*, and *Time Magazine* when preparing her speech on ethical issues relating to rap music.

The Speaking Requirements

You will give a number of public speeches in this class—your instructor will give you specific assignments. Although you will only speak for a total of around twenty-five minutes, you may face a lot of anxiety about those few minutes! Begin now to think of subjects that interest you. Read newspapers, listen to news reports, find fascinating topics in classes that you'd like to explore further. Be creative, and plan to learn a lot.

The Listening Requirements

Listening to the speeches of others is a vital part of learning to speak well. Following the examples of good models can help you become a better speaker; similarly, avoiding the mistakes of others will make you more effective. In addition, you will probably find that information from well-prepared speeches of your classmates will increase your understanding of the world in which you live.

Respectful listening to classmates is important, and as part of your classroom listening, you will probably be expected to participate in discussion of the speeches. For this reason, attendance is generally part of the course requirements.

The Writing Requirements

Quintilian believed that clear writing reflected clear thinking—which is another major goal of this course. Throughout the term, you will have many opportunities to show your clear thoughts and analytic skills in written assignments. In addition, a great deal of speaking in the world of work calls for a written as well as an oral report.

For these reasons, most instructors require outlines of your speeches, and both the text and this sourcebook present a number of examples that you can use as models. In addition, you will probably be asked to write a speaking outline for each speech—one that contains only cue words and phrases.

Throughout the quarter, you may also be asked to write in-class outlines and critiques of your fellow students' speeches. When you give them to your classmates, they provide very helpful feedback to the beginning speaker.

Ethical Public Speaking

Because public speaking has power to change the ideas and the behaviors of others, honesty is important in both listening and speaking. (See the text, pages 22–23, 129–131, and 154–157.) Occasionally students have crossed ethical boundaries—both unintentionally and intentionally, as these examples show:

- Two students worked together on a speech; each gave the speech, representing it as his own work. This is *plagiarism*.
- A student borrowed a speech from another dorm resident. Since it was the night before the speech, and time ran out, she copied the speech and gave it as her own. This is *plagiarism*.
- Another student used a speech from a file in his fraternity. He changed a few words, eliminated one main point, and rephrased one section entirely. But he submitted the ideas, general organizational pattern, and supporting materials of someone else. Again, this is *plagiarism*.
- A student cited sources that did not match the content of the speech. This is *fabrication*.

- Two students gave speeches on the same topic, which were quite different, as would be expected. However, both contained the exact wording on a point or two. Both students used one of the same sources. They both copied an example verbatim from that source. (Neither used quotation marks to indicate it was a direct quotation; neither cited the source.) This is *source plagiarism*.
- A student gave her outline to her friend who was desperate. This is *assisting in dishonesty*.

THE VALUE OF EFFECTIVE COMMUNICATION

Communication courses, such as public speaking, can benefit you in an "information society" that depends on your ability to send and to evaluate face-to-face, print, and mediated messages. Good communication skills are important in every major profession. Here are a just a few careers in which knowledge and skill in communication will enhance your career:

Business. Salesperson, manager, public relations officer, negotiator, employee trainer, personnel director, consultant.

Public Relations/Advertising. Publicity, advertising, marketing specialist, press agent, public opinion researcher.

Government. Politician, speechwriter, campaign director, legislative assistant, lobbyist, press secretary.

Law. Prosecutor, defense attorney, paralegal, legal educator, mediator, jury selection consultant.

Media. Reporter, scriptwriter, producer, filmmaker, media librarian, technician, researcher, director, editor.

Entertainment and Arts. Creative artist, business manager, author, promoter, public relations director, consultant, agent, fund-raiser.

Medicine. Health educator, public relations director, trainer, health counselor, drug rehabilitationist.

Education. Elementary, secondary, postsecondary teacher, speech pathologist, librarian, university recruiter, fund-raiser, safety educator (e.g. police officer, firefighter), park ranger, multicultural educator.

Social and Human Services. Minister, social worker, family counselor, human rights officer, community affairs specialist.

High Technology Industries. Producer or technician for closed-circuit TV or teleconference, performance assessor, speech synthesizer, researcher.

> **International Arenas**. Producer of information for international audiences, foreign correspondent, educator, humanitarian worker, international corporation representative, diplomat, negotiator, international relations specialist, tour coordinator.

Exercise 5, page 18, in the text directs you to this essay.

MERE LAW, MERE MEDICINE, MERE RHETORIC

Don Smith, University of New Haven

Although the study of public speaking has a long—and arguably proud—tradition, the term "rhetoric" is widely used in negative ways in this culture. That is, people often speak of "empty rhetoric," and they contrast rhetoric with action. In this essay, which appeared in the Eastern Communication Association Newsletter, Professor Smith discusses common misconceptions of the word "rhetoric" in U. S. public discourse.

If not Redecker then sooner or later some other reporter would have said it. The abuse is particularly apparent during the campaign years. Like millions of other Americans on February 6, 1992, my fiancee Barbara and I were sitting in the living room, eating dinner and watching the ABC evening news. Then Bill Redecker appeared with a report concerning American companies who recently struck successful business deals with Japan. "Reason not rhetoric," he announced, resulted in lucrative contracts with the Japanese.

What must viewers have thought? Whew?! Good thing those business leaders were smart enough to avoid rhetoric, that media buzzword denoting mere shallow, empty, flowery, bombastic, superficial, not to be trusted, spur of the moment, grab bag, tired, worn out, other than what he/she really meant, kind of speech. When rhetoric appears in the media, more often than not it is drawn in caricature, big mouth, small brain, dumbo ears, and beady eyes, just short of a clown hat and funny nose—a sad disposition for a term whose roots can be traced to the start of Western Civilization.

Worldwide there are thousands of people who have had formal training in the practice and analysis of rhetoric, a field that like medicine involves both science and art. In graduate classes these people have heard and now profess, as did Aristotle, that rhetoric is the "faculty of observing in any given case all the available means of persuasion"; that proper rhetorical practice is the result of ethical character, sound logic, and the appropriate use of emotional appeals; that each rhetor is duty-bound to know her subject and audience thoroughly, to find the right arguments and proofs, and to adapt her speech to that audience using whatever arrangement of ideas, style, and delivery is most appropriate. Students of Karl Wallace are reminded that good reason is the very substance of rhetoric.

One of the reasons that rhetoric is never discussed by reporters in terms of its full import is that the field can be quite complicated, and with a historical precedent of the term being used in a negative manner, it is easier for news, particularly television news, to apply the term to describe ineffective communicators and leave it at that. How would we explain to the general public in sixty seconds or less that the politician who says to his opponent, "Bill, that's just mere rhetoric," is himself employing a rhetorical strategy?

Perhaps we could explain it in this way. Rhetoric should be thought of as a protocol—a term familiar in medicine and the military. Were a patient to arrive at a hospital emergency room with an injured leg, the staff would react in a somewhat predictable manner. Questions would be asked to determine the how's and why's of the injury, the hand and eyes of a trained medical professional would examine the limb, and if an injury was suspected, only then would the leg be X-rayed. When the X-ray was interpreted the leg may or may not be set. Of one thing we can be certain: at any responsible hospital that leg would not be set willy-nilly into a cast without the proper questions being asked or the appropriate personnel having a look into the matter. To rush headlong into a procedure without the proper analysis would violate hospital protocol, that is, an established system for behaving in a given situation. A system is arrived at through the methodical study of situations that arise, the variables associated with them, the available choices, and the judgment of knowledgeable researchers and practitioners of the field as to what practice might best be employed.

To use the term rhetoric is also to imply the existence of systems or protocols associated with acts of human communication. Rhetoric may be employed to explain a particular response to a situation or to prescribe a response. Choosing one system over another doesn't necessarily guarantee success, but the goal of any good practitioner, pediatrician or rhetorician, is to come as close to success as the particular circumstances might allow and to adhere to the code of ethics that govern his or her practice.

Malpractice can be found in any field, but while a snake oil salesman might profess to be a doctor and sell something that purports to be medicine, we do not judge an entire profession by that person's delusional behavior. It would be nice if the news media would make a more conscientious effort to accord this same courtesy to the professional researchers and practitioners of rhetoric who work in this country and who occasionally have dinner while watching the evening news.

Discussion Questions

1. What are your ideas about "rhetoric"?
2. How does Smith (and Aristotle) define rhetoric?

3. How, according to Smith, is rhetoric like medicine?

4. Can you think of instances of public speakers who should be accused of "rhetorical malpractice"?

SPEECH ASSIGNMENT:
Telling a Modern Legend

Time: 1½–3 minutes

Description

Introduce yourself to your classmates by telling a legend that has been handed down from either your *family* or from a *significant group* to which you belong such as your sports team, living group, religious group, club, or place of work. You may choose one of the oral stories from exercise 4, page 18 of the text. The speech consists of two parts:

Part 1: The story itself takes most of the time of the speech.

Part 2: The main lesson of the story reveals some of your personal traits or the values you believe are important.

Skills

Select a story appropriate to the assignment and time limitations.
Identify the point of the story and link that point to yourself.
Introduce and conclude the story in an interesting manner.
Survive!!

Guidelines

1. Select a legend that is appropriate to the audience. Consider the complexity of the story. Can it be told within the short time period? Does your audience have enough background knowledge so the story will make sense to them? What does the story reveal about your personality?

2. List the events of the story in chronological order. Include any relevant details that the audience needs to understand the narrative. After you have the main events in order, go through and edit irrelevant details that do not contribute to the point of the story.

3. Write out the point of the story and the characteristics it reveals about your family or group. Link those characteristics to yourself.

4. Plan an opening statement that will get the audience's attention to your topic. DO NOT say, "I'm gonna tell a story about my grandma." Here are a few suggestions:

   • Start your story with a specific time and place. "When my grandmother was twelve years old, she sailed to the United States alone."

   • Start with a short quotation that tells the moral of your story. "They say that only the good die young; one of my soccer team's heroes proves that saying."

5. Write key *words* on a note card so that you can jog your memory during your speech. Do not write out the speech word for word. Do not try to memorize the speech.

6. Rehearse the main ideas of the speech. Select the exact wording only as you rehearse. Your speech should sound just a little bit different each time.

SAMPLE SPEECH:
Self-Introduction

I'm from the South; and if you come from the South, or know anything about the South, you'll know how important good cooking is to a Southerner. Eating meals together is a tradition in my family. Every holiday of my childhood was spent over a meal at my grandparents' home, enjoying my grandmother's cooking. Hand in hand with the meal was storytelling—my grandfather being the center of storytelling attention. He told stories about everything: the family murders, people in the neighborhood, his childhood, and even stories about food!

One story I remember in particular was one he told about some of his experiences as a child during the Great Depression. After our meal was finished, he'd push back his chair, look at me, and begin.

"Boy," he'd say, "let me tell you 'bout when I was comin' up. You think you got it hard now, but I say you all got it easy. When I was a boy—during the Depression—we didn't have none of this here fancy food. Just potatoes!

Baked potatoes,
       boiled potatoes,
              creamed potatoes,
                     mashed potatoes,
                            potato salad,
                                   potato soup . . .

Biscuits too, if we was lucky. Nothin' better than momma's warm biscuit with a bit of butter. Course no one had no butter then. But IF you did, you gave thanks. You gave thanks to the good Lord no matter what ya had," he'd tell me.

"Give thanks," he commanded me throughout my life, and accompanying this advice was the example of his life lived in thanks. His thankfulness never stopped when the meal was finished and the food cleared away. Instead, he was grateful throughout all aspects of his life. My grandfather's life—and this story he tells—illustrate for me what it is to be thankful. Through his example, I have learned to be thankful for what I am given.

(Story told by Derek Reamy, Loyola University, Maryland)

EVALUATION FORM

Modern Legend

Time: 1½–3 minutes

Name_____Time _____

___Story appropriate to the assignment

___Interesting opening statement

___Understandable order of events

___Edited; all material relevant

___Point of story is clear

___Point is linked to speaker

Delivery

(Your instructor will describe your behaviors such as eye contact, posture and gestures, use of your voice.)

Memory

_____   Obviously well rehearsed

_____   Use of one note card only; no complete sentences

Grade_____

2

Overview of the Speechmaking Process

(Use with exercise 1, page 40.)

TOPIC QUESTIONNAIRE

At the outset of the term it is helpful to identify possible topics so that you can be alert for material throughout the term. The following exercises can help you begin the process of topic selection.

What traits do you admire in people? What people embody these traits? Which of these people might you develop a speech about?

What courses have you enjoyed most? What possible topics are in those subjects?

What experiences have you had that might lead to speech topics?

hobbies?

job related?

health related?

recreational pursuits?

Check any interesting areas relating to issues and policies that you can use to brainstorm further narrowed topics:

___ Freedom of Speech (flag burning, harassment, censorship)

___ Crime (prevention, punishment, prisoner lawsuits, drug war)

___ Civil rights (rights of women and minorities, international rights)

___ Weapons (metal detectors, nuclear, historical weapons, car bombs)

___ Personal (health, self-defense, job security, time management)

___ Privacy issues (personal data on computers, caller ID, lifestyles)

___ Psychology (personality theories, memories, defense mechanisms)

___ Entertainment (violent video games, sports salaries, cable TV)

A public speaking class is a good time to explore international or cultural topics. Check all the areas that interest you—even slightly. Make a mind map (consider history, politics, cultural traditions, famous people, tourist sites, etc.) showing narrowed topics you might use in a classroom speech.

___African nations	___International business	___Oceania
___Central America	___South America	___Europe
___Russia	___Native Americans	___Australia
___Middle East	___Ethnic traditions	___Asia

WORKSHEET:
Purpose Statements and Central Idea

Write purpose statements and central ideas for each outline of main points. (For use with Chapter 2, pages 29–32.)

I. General Purpose:

Specific Purpose:

Central Idea:

Main Points: A. Face-lifts are common cosmetic surgeries.
B. Many people have their noses reconstructed.
C. Chin augmentation is a type of plastic surgery.

II. General Purpose:

Specific Purpose:

Central Idea:

Main Points: A. Healthy blood donors are always needed.
B. It takes a minimum of effort to donate blood.
C. Your reward is knowing you helped someone.
D. Donate today at the bloodmobile on campus.

III. General Purpose:

Specific Purpose:

Central Idea:

Main Points: 1. Chinese writing has pictures of objects.
2. Some symbols are ideas in picture form.
3. Some represent abstract ideas.
4. Other words stand for lessons.

IV. General Purpose:

Specific Purpose:

Central Idea:

Main Points: A. First is the transition from drowsiness to sleep.
B. It's easy to awaken in the next stage—light sleep.
C. The third and fourth stages are called deep sleep.
D. Vivid dreams occur in REM (rapid eye movement) sleep.

SPEECH ASSIGNMENT:
Single Point Speech

Time: 2–3 minutes

Definition

A single point speech is one in which you present only one major idea and develop it with several pieces of supporting information. See the sample speech by Andrés Lucero on pages 39–40 in the text.

Skills

Ability to state a major idea
Ability to state and explain reasons that support your idea
Brief introduction and memorable conclusion
Selection of appropriate language
Extemporaneous delivery

Guidelines

1. Select one idea that you can support. Suggestions: Vacations are important. Volunteering to coach in the Special Olympics enriched my life. There are three good reasons NOT to cohabitate before marriage.

2. Provide reasons such as examples, facts, and statistics to support your major idea. You may have to do library research, interview a knowledgeable person, draw from your own experiences, or use electronically stored data as you gather your supporting materials.

3. Plan a brief introduction to orient your audience to your topic.

4. Think the speech through to a concluding statement.

5. Rehearse the speech. Do not memorize exact wording; instead, learn only the major ideas and the relationship between them. Put key words on note cards so that you can use them as you speak.

Example of a brief outline of the ideas in a single point speech. (Note: Each point is explained in greater detail in the actual speech.)

Introduction: When I first entered college, I had not declared a major, and I went through my first year taking core courses. However, I got tired of hearing people (my mother) ask me what I was going to do with my life, so I began to focus on a major.

[Single point]: I decided that a communication major was right for me.

First reason: The communication department is in the college of liberal arts, and a liberal arts degree provides a good foundation for a number of careers—as well as for the career changes we can expect throughout our lifetimes.

Second reason: I became convinced that communication is increasingly important, not only in this culture, but in a global culture that is increasingly linked by technology.

Third reason: The communication department offers interesting courses that will help me in my future career. Besides public speaking, there are courses in interpersonal, intercultural, small group, organizational, and nonverbal communication.

Conclusion: Now, my mom no longer asks what I plan to do. She just waits for the day I get my first paycheck.

EVALUATION FORM

Single Point Speech

Name_____ Time _____

Major Point of Speech

____ Gains attention in introduction

____ Single point clearly stated

____ Reasons clearly stated

____ Each reason explained

____ Memorable concluding statement

____ Appropriate language

Delivery

____ Evidence of practice

____ Minimal use of note cards

Grade _____

3

Public Speaking and Culture

EXPLORE YOUR PERSONAL VALUES

Milton Rokeach identified two basic types of values: instrumental and terminal values. *Instrumental values* are *behaviors* considered important as "means" or instruments to reach a "good" and worthwhile society. Some are *moral* values by which we relate to others; and others are *competence* values related to our individual personalities. *Terminal values* are the *goals* or ideals that are important "ends" in societies. Some of these have a *social focus,* and others have a *personal focus.*

Many scholars have made lists of "American" values. The following list combines items from several lists. Select five values that are very significant to you personally, then select five that are least important. Discuss your choices with a small group of your classmates.

___Ambition	___Politeness	___Tolerance
___Honesty	___Individuality	___Equality
___Freedom	___Hard work	___Success
___An optimistic outlook	___Achievement of goals	___Efficiency and practicality
___Cleanliness	___Patriotism	___Helping others
___Orderliness	___A happy family	___Change, progress
___Courage	___Forgiveness	___Wisdom
___Creativity	___Self-control	___Self-reliance
___Dependablity	___Friendship	___World peace
___Prosperous life	___Happiness	___Inner peace
___Pleasure	___Self-esteem	___An exciting life

- Which of these values do you think are moral?
- Which make you more competent?
- Which are social? (Are paid for with tax money?)
- Which make you a better person?
- How did you learn these values?

━━━━━━━━

SPEECH ASSIGNMENT:
A Tribute

2–3 minutes

Definition

A tribute is a special kind of ceremonial speech that praises characteristics of people who exemplify important cultural traits.

Skills

Identify an important cultural belief, value, attitude, or behavior.
Identify a person who embodies that cultural resource.
Prepare a speech of praise that reinforces the importance of the belief, value, attitude, or behavior.
Prepare an introduction and conclusion for your speech.

Guidelines

1. Choose a worthy subject, contemporary or historical, who embodies characteristics and values that are positive and worthy of admiration and emulation by others in the society. Heroes—famous or lesser known—come from many fields such as medicine, education, politics, and religion.

2. Arrange your speech into an introduction, body, and conclusion:

    a. Introduce your subject creatively by planning an interesting opening line. For example, instead of saying, "Today I am going to talk about Jimmy Carter," narrate a story of the ex-president's work with Habitat for Humanity, a nonprofit group that helps poor people build their own homes. For a tribute to the late artist Georgia O'Keefe, begin with a quotation from the *New York Times*'s obituary that praised her work. After the opening statement, provide enough information for the audience to understand who your subject is and why this person deserves praise.

    b. The major part of your speech reveals the traits that are worthy of emulation by others in the society. Include some or all of these elements:

    Background—parentage, hardships, ethnic roots, and so on.

    Education—educational background, whether positive or negative.

    Achievements—character traits that are worthy of discussion. Look for traits in three areas: personality (such as friendliness or curiosity), physical attributes (such as speed or endurance), and characteristics of the spirit (such as courage or perseverance). Include examples that demonstrate your subject's character. Summarize the subject's lasting achievements or enduring legacy.

c. Think your speech through to the very end. Conclude with a summary of the major values embodied in the life of your character, values that other people can emulate. Finish, as you began, with a memorable statement.

A TRIBUTE TO THE DOG

George Graham Vest

A speech of praise does not have to focus specifically on people. Speakers also praise ideas such as "justice" or "liberty." They also praise animals that exhibit traits that are important. This speech is given in praise of a dog. The speaker, George Graham Vest (1830–1904), was a lawyer in a small Missouri town where one man sued another for killing his dog. Vest represented the plaintiff. This is his summation speech to the jury. As you might guess, his client won the case. Vest went on to become a U.S. senator from Missouri from 1879 to 1903.

This speech was given over 100 years ago. As you read through it, notice the changes in language that have occurred in the century. For one thing, "he" is used as a generic pronoun. In addition, compare this to the informality of style in the speech on drums found at the end of Chapter 11.

GENTLEMEN OF THE JURY: The best friend a man has in the world may turn against him and become his enemy. His son or daughter that he has reared with loving care may prove ungrateful. Those who are nearest and dearest to us, those whom we trust with our happiness and our good name may become traitors to their faith. The money that a man has, he may lose. It flies away from him, perhaps when he needs it most. A man's reputation may be sacrificed in a moment of ill-considered action. The people who are prone to fall on their knees to do us honor when success is with us may be the first to throw the stone of malice when failure settles its cloud upon our heads.

The one absolutely unselfish friend that man can have in this selfish world, the one that never deserts him, the one that never proves ungrateful or treacherous is his dog. A man's dog stands by him in prosperity and in poverty, in health and in sickness. He will sleep on the cold ground, where the wintry winds blow and the snow drives fiercely, if only he may be near his master's side. He will kiss the hand that has no food to offer; he will lick the wounds and sores that come in encounter with the roughness of the world. He guards the sleep of his pauper master as if he were a prince. When all other friends desert, he remains. When riches take wings and reputation falls to pieces, he is as constant in his love as the sun in its journey through the heavens.

If fortune drives the master forth an outcast in the world, friendless and homeless, the faithful dog asks no higher privilege than that of accompanying him, to guard him against danger, to fight against his enemies. And when the last scene of all comes, and death takes his master in its embrace and his body is laid away in the cold ground, no matter if all other friends pursue their way, there by the graveside will the noble dog be found, his head between his paws, his eyes sad but open in alert watchfulness, faithful and true even in death.

Discussion Questions

1. What characteristics of the dog does Vest praise? What would our society be like if more people behaved as Vest argues a dog behaves?

2. Do you know of a person who would be a good topic for a speech because he or she embodies the same characteristics that Vest praises?

EVALUATION FORM

Speech of Tribute

Name_____ Time _____

____Person introduced clearly
____Background information adequate
____Education described
____Achievements identified
   ____of the spirit
   ____of the body
   ____of fortune
____Compared with another (optional)

Editing

____All points relevant?
____Character clearly defined
____Unity of speech

Organization

____Began with impact
____Ended with impact

Cultural Values

____Clearly identified
____Relevant to this audience
____Embodied in the subject

Delivery

____Minimal use of note cards
____Direct eye contact
____Posture and gestures appropriate
____Conversational
____Fluency of thought

Grade____

4

Communicative Competence

WORKSHEET:
Your Communicative Competence

How do you feel about taking this class?

What public speaking experiences have you had?

- How well did you do? How do you know?

- How did your listeners respond to your speech(es)?

Draw the diagram on page 71 showing motivation, knowledge, and skills. In each circle evaluate what do you do well and where you need improvement. (Example: In the knowledge circle, you know how to choose a topic, and you need to improve in your research.)

What are your personal goals for the class; that is, what do you want to get out of the course?

How can you best meet these goals?

![CHECKLIST]

CHECKLIST

Read through this checklist before your next speech. After your speech, fill it in. Then try to analyze your stress management and think of one area you can improve for your next speech assignment.

Write *B* (before), *D* (during), or *A* (after) to document what you did to take active control of your speaking experience.

PHYSICAL   _____ Took deep breaths

                _____ Went for a run

                _____ Ate sensibly

                _____ Consciously relaxed my muscles

                _____ Got a drink

MENTAL   _____ Studied the organizational pattern for the speech

                _____ Thought about my topic and how important it is

                _____ Thought, "I can do this. I will do well."

                _____ Visualized myself giving an effective speech

                _____ Prepared well in advance

EMOTIONAL   _____ Selected a topic that I enjoyed

                _____ Realized that my performance does not relate to my value as a person

                _____ Thought, "I have done a good job preparing."

                _____ Enjoyed the positive reaction of my classmates

1. What personal goals did you set?

2. Did you meet them?

3. How did the audience respond to you?

4. Did you feel competent that you knew how to prepare the assigned speech? If not, what did you not know? What steps can you take to learn the process better?

5

Speakers and Pluralistic Audiences

AUDIENCE WORKSHEET

Before any speech, it is a good idea to sit down with a paper and pencil and jot down some impressions about your audience. You might want to use a form such as this.

1. What kind of audience is this primarily?

    ___Pedestrian

    ___Passive

    ___Voluntary

    ___Concerted

    ___Organized

2. Knowing this, what is your major challenge? (See the "Key Concepts" box on page 97.)

3. What common concerns do you and your listeners face? What common interests do you have? What illustrations and examples are familiar to both you and your audience? Use the following categories to identify some of these areas of common ground. (Figure 14.1 on page 319 in the text shows a diagram of these categories and their relationship to audience interests.)

    Campus

    Local

    State

    Regional

    National

    International

4. How can you find out how your audience feels about your topic?

THE CLASSROOM AUDIENCE

In order to participate in a "dialogue" with your classroom audience, learn as much about your fellow classmates as you can by thinking dialogically before, during, and after your speech.

Before the Speech

1. *Observations.* You have already gathered information by observation. For instance, you know the sex, race, and approximate ages of your classmates. The clothing and accessories of individuals provide additional information about them. Do any wear religious symbols? Engagement or wedding rings? Does clothing reflect interest—such as support for a cause, membership in a sorority, or affiliation with a sports team? What other courses are some of them taking as indicated by the titles of books they carry? Do any ride bicycles to class? All of these observable features can provide you with clues about common interests and points of difference between you and your audience.

2. *Interactions.* You can also gain information by conversing with your fellow students before or after class. Simply approach one or two other students and ask if you can discuss a possible topic. Generally, most students are willing to answer questions.

   • Ask a general question first, something like, "What do you know about prisoners' lawsuits?" If they know everything about the issue, you probably do not have a good speech topic.

   • However, if they are relatively unfamiliar with the topic, ask another question such as, "When, if ever, should a prisoner sue the government?"

   • You might follow with, "How do you feel when you find out that a prisoner sued because he was given creamy peanut butter instead of chunky—and such lawsuits take millions of tax dollars annually?"

   By focusing your questions, you can get a fairly good idea about your classmates' knowledge and interests. This will help you relate to their here-and-now concerns.

3. *Questionnaires.* You can ask for written information by distributing questionnaires. You will probably use a combination of three common types of questions used on questionnaires: closed, open, and scaled questions. (See also pages 127–128 in the text.)

   Closed questions require a simple yes or no answer or a specific, short response, as these examples demonstrate:

Do you favor lifetime imprisonment for criminals after they are convicted of three major crimes?

___Yes

___No

___I do not have enough information to respond.

Where did you graduate from high school?_____

What is your major?_____

Open questions allow your listeners to write their answer in their own words, expressing their personal opinions. Such questions may help you target specific misconceptions your classmates have or areas in which they have little information. Some examples of open questions are:

What do you think are the advantages and disadvantages of hair replacement techniques?

Why do you think people join the Peace Corps?

Scaled questions allow listeners to respond across a continuum or scale. They are often helpful for gathering information on the relative strength of beliefs, values, and attitudes. Thus, if you want to know the strength of your audience's involvement with your topic, use scaled questions such as these:

Most college students would cheat if they could.

I————I————I————I————I————I————I

| strongly agree | agree | mildly agree | no opinion | mildly disagree | disagree | strongly disagree |

I write letters to my congressional representative.

I————I————I————I————I

| never | rarely | occasionally | often | regularly |

Pornography is:

I————I————I————I————I————I————I

| highly moral | moral | somewhat moral (OK) | no opinion | somewhat immoral | immoral | highly immoral |

There is an example of a combination questionnaire on page 35. The initial series of closed questions helps you identify characteristics that may influence how classmates respond to your topic. The scaled questions help you assess the intensity of their attitudes. The final questions allow them to discuss the issues in their own words.

After the Speech

Although you as speaker take most of the responsibility for preparing the message, you stand the risk of being misunderstood. Therefore, when possible, provide the audience an opportunity to engage in public dialogue with you by asking questions. This also provides you with an opportunity to restate your main points and clarify and amplify the ideas you presented.

Here are some tips you can use for a question and answer session:

1. *Prepare for questions.* Try to anticipate areas where the audience may have questions, and do enough research so that you feel confident in these problematic areas.

2. *Don't expect to know everything.* It is all right to admit that you don't have all the answers, so don't try to bluff through an answer. Say instead, "I'll check that and get back to you." (Then do so.)

3. *Consider the audience as a whole.* One questioner may ask a question that is not of general interest to the entire group. Although the questioner is interested, the rest of the audience is left out of the dialogue. If you recognize this is happening, make arrangements to meet the individual after the speech to continue the discussion.

4. *Prepare for disagreement.* Some listeners may disagree publicly. Welcome diverse opinions, but don't allow a hostile or negative questioner to throw you off balance. Arrange to discuss differences after the speech.

5. *Invite listeners to add information and illustrations that will elaborate on your ideas.* This is an additional way you can cooperate with your audience to co-create meaning. For example, someone may have taken a course, seen a television program, read an article, or had an experience related to your topic. By contributing this information, individual audience members help the entire audience gain a more complete understanding of your subject.

See M. Martel (1984). *Before you say a word: The executive's guide to effective communication.* Englewood Cliffs, NJ: Prentice-Hall.

A COMBINATION QUESTIONNAIRE

Name (optional)_____

Age _____   Sex_____   Major_____

Have you ever been the object of hate speech?

___yes ___no ___don't know

Place an X on the point of the scale that best indicates your response to the sentence:

SA	=	strongly agree	
A	=	agree	
MA	=	mildly agree	
N	=	no opinion	

MD	=	mildly disagree
D	=	disagree
SD	=	strongly disagree

Hate speech should be banned on campus.

I————————I————————I————————I————————I————————I————————I

SA   A   MA   N   MD   D   SD

Anyone who engages in hate speech should attend compulsory sensitivity training sessions.

I————————I————————I————————I————————I————————I————————I

SA   A   MA   N   MD   D   SD

Some kinds of hate speech are worse than others.

I————————I————————I————————I————————I————————I————————I

SA   A   MA   N   MD   D   SD

How would you define hate speech?

What effect do you think it has on its victims?

What is the best way to deal with it on campus?

What kinds of hate speech, if any, are worse than others?

6

Listening

LISTENING SELF-EVALUATION:
Before, During, and After the Speech

Name of Speaker _____

Topic_____

Before the Speech

I know a lot about this topic already.

I————————I————————I————————I————————I
Strongly   Agree   No Opinion   Disagree   Strongly
Agree   Disagree

I want to hear more about this subject.

I————————I————————I————————I————————I
SA   A   N   D   SD

This topic is significant to my personal life.

I————————I————————I————————I————————I
SA   A   N   D   SD

During the Speech

I have these questions (use closed, open, clarification, request for specific information, request for elaboration).

After the Speech

I agreed with this speaker.

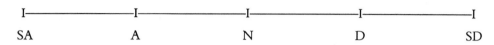

SA   A   N   D   SD

I was able to detect the speaker's biases or prejudices.

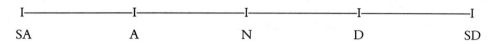

SA   A   N   D   SD

I listened in order to distinguish facts from opinions.

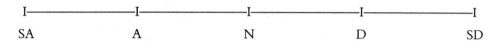

SA   A   N   D   SD

I found myself distracted by the speaker's personal mannerisms.

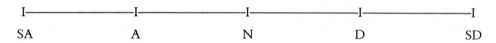

SA   A   N   D   SD

I did well in these areas:

I need to improve in these areas:

SPEECH CRITIQUE GUIDELINES

Evaluate the speeches of your classmates, using the five canons of rhetoric as a guide.

In the canon of invention:

__Topic (appropriate? need to address the topic?)

__Evidence of research (sources cited? credible sources? major points supported with credible data?)

__Sensitivity to audience (meets their needs? deals with possible objections? respectful? etc.)

__"Good reasons" given for major ideas? (reasoning sound? emotional proofs used well? speaker is credible?)

In the canon of disposition or organization:

__Introduction (all the parts included? is the intro effective?)

__Body (organizational pattern? is it effective?)

__Conclusion (all parts here? is the conclusion effective?)

In the canon of style:

__Clear (avoids or defines jargon?)

__Interesting (metaphors? repetition? vivid words? etc.)

__Connotative words (effective?)

__Avoids demeaning terminology

__Concise

In the canon of memory:

__Knew major ideas

__Few references to notes

In the canon of delivery:

__Eye contact (inclusive?)

__Appearance (appropriate grooming? clothing? accessories?)

__Voice (effective vocal variety? use of pauses? rate? volume?)

__Time (within limits?)

Especially effective:

Suggestions for improvement:

SAMPLE CRITIQUE

Invention:

—Well-chosen topic. I thought I knew about coffee, but you showed me how much more I had to learn.

—Good adaptation to non-coffee drinkers—a major industry with more workers than any other.

—Great facts—from the discovery in Ethiopia, the spread through Africa and into the Muslim culture, then throughout the world. Citing sources = good.

—Visuals well used. Thanks for the sample!

—Kept my interest. Beethoven really counted 60 beans/cup?!

Organization:

—Intro: What is your link to the subject?

—Basically topical with chronological subpoint.

—In chronological point—the map helped us see how it spread over time throughout the world.

—Points = easy to distinguish—your preview helped us.

—Some repetition in the conclusion—summary = very detailed.

Style:

—Watch "me and my family." It's "my family and I."

—I liked the vivid descriptions of coffee plants and beans.

Memory:

—Close tie to notes in introduction, but better as you went along.

Delivery:

—Eye contact sometimes to the instructor, but generally good.

—Your gestures = illustrators

—Fast in places

Especially Effective:

—Keep up the interesting topics and continue to do the kind of research that really adds to our knowledge!

Suggestions for Improvement:

—Look again at both the introduction and conclusion to make sure you link yourself to the topic and review only briefly.

UNIT II

Principles in the Five Canons of Rhetoric

7

Researching the Speech

LIBRARY WORKSHEET

Author Search

Find a book by Deborah Tannen. Write the call letters in this space._____
Use correct bibliographic form to cite it, following this example.

Author's last name, first initial. middle initial. (date). Title, underlined, with only the first word, proper nouns, and the first word of the subtitle capitalized. City of publication: Company.

_____

_____

_____

Subject Search

Book. Subject of crime. Call letters: _____Cite correctly, using the pattern for bibliographic citation shown above:

_____

_____

_____

Magazine or Journal Article

Subject: gun control. Follow this form to cite it:

Author(s)' last name, first initial. middle initial. (year, month [day]). Title—capitalized as noted above. Magazine title underlined, volume underlined, page number(s).

_____

_____

Newspaper Article

Subject: gun control; follow this source citation format:

Author(s)' last name, first initial. middle initial. (year, month day). Title. Newspaper title underlined, p. number(s).

_____

_____

_____

Electronically Stored Data

Find a television program on anorexia or bulimia.

Last name, first initial. middle initial. (Producer). & last name, first initial. middle initial. (Director). (date). Title underlined. [Television program]. Company.

_____

_____

_____

Reference Section

Write the title of the most intriguing dictionary you can find. [examples: *New dictionary of American slang; A dictionary of pianists*]

_____

Write an interesting encyclopedia title. [examples: *The encyclopedia of phobias, fears, and anxieties. The encyclopedia of music in Canada*]

_____

If a computer encyclopedia is available in your library, spend some time searching for topics that interest you. Jot down notes on what you did.

COMPUTER TOPIC SEARCH

1. *Purpose and Scope of Search.* Before you sit down at the computer to do a subject search, summarize your topic as completely and concisely as possible. For example:

   What has been the effect of computers on banking techniques both nationally and internationally?

   Now, summarize your search topic in one or two sentences.

   _____

   _____

2. *Identify Main Concepts.* Underline or circle the main concepts in your summary statement. For example:

   What has been the effect of <u>computers</u> on <u>banking techniques</u> both nationally and internationally?

3. *Select Subject Terms.* List the terms that describe your main concepts. Ask a reference librarian for the guide *Search INFORM*, which will identify appropriate terms for a computer search. For example:

First term(s)	*Second term(s)*	*Third term(s)*
computers	banking	techniques
or	or	or
minicomputers	banks	methods
or	or	or
microcomputers	international banking	procedures

Now, enter the subject terms for your computer search:

First term(s)	*Second term(s)*	*Third term(s)*
_____	_____	_____
or	or	or
_____	_____	_____
or	or	or
_____	_____	_____

Adapted from a worksheet prepared by Joan D'Andrea, St. John's University librarian.

8

Supporting Materials

FACT–OPINION WORKSHEET

Write "F" beside factual statements and "O" beside statements of opinion.

Illegal Childcare Workers

___The number of illegal workers is anybody's guess. But, says Lisa Schanzer of Family Extensions, Inc., a Connecticut placement agency, "If you sent every illegal [nanny] in this country home, you'd have a disaster overnight."

___A Jamaican nanny says, "Americans say, West Indians come and take our jobs. But would they do this work? A lot of Americans aren't into baby-sitting. They'd rather go to the office."

Source: Melinda Beck et al. (1993, February 22). Mary Poppins speaks out. *Newsweek,* pp. 66, 67.

Feline Leukemia Virus Infection

___Feline leukemia virus is not at all hardy. It can survive only two to three minutes in air and only two to three days in a moist environment other than living cells.

___Many public health officials and FeLV researchers, however, believe the safest policy at this time is strict isolation of any cat diagnosed as FeLV-infected.

___Vaccination with "Leukocell" is recommended for all healthy cats nine weeks of age or older.

___First-time vaccination requires two doses given two to three weeks apart and a booster dose given two to four months later.

Source: *Feline Leukemia Virus Infection: Life-saving information for cat owners* (brochure). Lincoln, NE: Norden Laboratories.

MTV: Beavis and Butthead

____ You never see either of them without the other, and parents or siblings are nowhere to be found.

____ The humor of *Beavis and Butthead* is subtle and intangible. Either you respond or you don't.

____ Crudely drawn cartoon adolescents, the blond-haired Beavis and the brown-haired Butthead are neither intelligent nor glamorous nor attractive.

____ I, together with millions of other Americans, like Beavis and Butthead.

Source: James Gardner (1994, May 2). *National Review*, pp. 60–62.

TESTING EVIDENCE

Facts

A speech, "Brother Eagle, Sister Sky," is commonly attributed to Chief Seattle. It is widely quoted and is the subject of a children's book "by" Chief Seattle. The speech was actually written in 1972 by a screenwriter named Ted Perry for a film about ecology.

- *How might you find out that the speech was not, in fact, written by Chief Seattle and thus avoid perpetuating misinformation?*

One speaker, arguing that Mexican factories were controlled by managers who exploited workers, said that management walked into a factory in Mexico one day and began shooting and killing workers. In truth, managers were not involved in the incident at all. Union members did the shooting—and no one was killed. Put simply, the true story had to do with union–worker disputes, not management–worker exploitation.

- *Why do you think the speaker told a story that was not true?*
- *How might he have avoided this falsehood?*

Examples

In the early 1990s, Kimberly Bergalis died after contracting AIDS allegedly from her dentist. She testified before Congress urging that laws be passed to test health care workers for AIDS. She and six other patients of the same dentist are the only cases in the United States of infection transmitted by this route. Further inquiry has revealed that each of the six might have had other transmission routes. Since the dentist is dead, he cannot defend himself.

• *Does Ms. Bergalis pass the tests, and thus become a good example?*

In 1993, one abortion protester shot and killed a doctor who performed abortions; a woman shot and wounded another. In 1994, a third shot and killed an abortion provider and his escort.

• *Are there a sufficient number of shootings of abortion providers to use these incidents as an illustration of typical violence directed against clinics?*
• *What is the effect of using an example that is extreme but possible?*
• *What forms of violence against abortion providers are most typical?*

Testimony

Dr. Robert Coles, a Harvard professor, is well known for his scholarly work on children—their moral and religious development, their adjustment to poverty. He has written and lectured widely on these subjects.

• On what topics might you quote Dr. Coles?
• How would you evaluate a speaker who said, "Dr. Coles, a Harvard professor, is concerned about global warming?"

Reporters wrote that radio personality Rush Limbaugh admitted he is not very well read in history. It is true that Limbaugh admitted his lack of historical knowledge, but the larger context for his remark was that Americans as a whole know little about history, and he would like to be better read in the subject.

• *Assess the reporters' use of this evidence.*

Quantification

The Princeton Dental Resource Center provides newsletters for dentists to distribute to patients. One issue contained the startling claim that eating chocolate might aid in keeping plaque bacteria down. Some researchers, studying the relationship between different foods and cavities, found chocolate bars to produce only 72 percent as many cavities as pure sugar caused. The Princeton group (run by two dentists) failed to report that they received about 90 percent of their million-dollar budget from a candy company.

• *What test(s) for quantification does this study fail to meet?*

In the first quarter of 1993, health officials reported a 204 percent increase in the number of AIDS cases over the number reported during the same quarter in

1992. However, on January 1, 1993, federal health officials expanded the definition of AIDS to include twenty-seven conditions instead of the twenty-three that formerly signaled the presence of the disease. Some of the new conditions were primarily associated with women.

Federal officials attributed some of the increase to the possibility that certain state and local health officials waited until the new definition went into effect before reporting their new cases.

- *Knowing that the definition for AIDS was changed as of 1/1/93, how should you compare AIDS statistics from the 1980s and the 1990s?*
- *How might a speaker who didn't do enough research to know that the definition was changed mislead listeners regarding women and the incidence of AIDS?*

Comparison

Drug prevention = a war

Teen pregnancy = a floodtide

Unresolved tribal issues in a certain African nation = a time bomb waiting to go off

A new candidate = a breath of fresh air

- *Such figurative comparisons as these are common. Examine each one and evaluate if the comparison makes sense to you.*

Hillary Clinton is like Eleanor Roosevelt.

The parking problems at your school are like the parking problems at University X (a larger school in an urban setting).

Cuban refugees are like Haitian refugees.

- *Here you are literally comparing two like things. What is the major test for this type of evidence? Do these examples pass the test?*

9

Organizing the Speech

SPEECH OUTLINE: THE SPIRAL PATTERN

Conclusion: As you can see, Lincoln's years at the university were essentially wasted. Although he had a lot of fun and made many friends, his lack of career planning has left him in a frustrating job with very little chance to fulfill his dreams of success.

Janelle, on the other hand, caught herself early enough to begin setting goals and working toward them. The result is that, after a brief period, she was able to get a job that is satisfactory to her.

Tamara followed the ideal way to use college as a stepping stone to her career. By following her example—or that of Janelle—you too can take the important steps necessary to begin your career effectively.

- Got out and immediately went to work in a job she liked.
- Built a placement file as she went.
- Developed interviewing skills.
- Did an internship to build a network outside the university.
- Planned her coursework carefully.
  —Did not avoid challenging courses.
  —Took courses in the liberal arts that would prepare her for any career changes that might be in her future.
- Maintained a good grade point average from her first year.

(Cycle 3) Tamara planned from her first year to make the most of her college experience.

- As a result, she worked in a low-paying job for a few months but found a better job within a short period of time.
- Began during her senior year to contact the career placement center, build a file, and construct a resume.
- She worked hard to improve her GPA.

(Cycle 2) Janelle began to get serious about school during her junior year.

- He may even have to return to school.
- He is now beginning to think about writing a resume.
- After college he took a poorly paying job with no future.
- Even with an "easy" major, his GPA was low.
- He chose a major and took courses that were reportedly easy.

(Cycle 1) Lincoln never got serious about academics.

Introduction: All of us are first- and second-year students, and—regardless of the fun we are having at college—our major reason for being here is to gain marketable skills that will enable us to get a well-paying job.

Three of my friends recently graduated, and their stories can give us some guidelines for planning our own career track.

CONNECTING THE PARTS OF THE SPEECH

Below you will find a speech outline. Work with another member of the class to write connectives between the parts of the speech. For example, where the directions say [signpost] use the information in the central idea to write a signpost that introduces the main point.

Introduction:

A. On November 10, 1984, I arrived in the United States to meet my adoptive family.

B. Someday you may be in the position of adopting a child.

C. I was adopted when I was a teenager.

D. Today, I will discuss the four steps for adopting a child from another country: application, selection of child, child arrival, and postplacement.

Body:

A. [Signpost]_____Application.

1. The agency sends information.

2. You fill in an application.

3. The agency evaluates your suitability to adopt.

B. [Signpost] _____Selection.

1. Your name goes on a waiting list.

2. A social worker sends pictures and information about a child.

3. You select a child and sign a Placement Agreement Form.

[Transition]:_____

C. Child Arrival.

1. Apply for an "Orphan Visa" to bring your child into the United States.

2. An escort brings the child (and other children) to the United States.

3. The family gets medical insurance for the child.

[Internal Summary]:_____

D. Postplacement.

1. For six months to a year, the social worker works with your family.

2. The child is legally adopted.

Conclusion:

A. In conclusion, application, selection, child arrival, and postplacement are the steps you go through in adopting a child from overseas.

B. Although this may seem like a lot of work, I am grateful that my parents did it.

C. Without them, I would probably still be in an orphanage in the Philippines.

Source: Cribbins, Marieta (1991, January 22). The adoption process. Student speech, Oregon State University.

CONTENT OUTLINE FORMAT

This is the typical linear outline format that many speech instructors require. Use this general form to outline the contents of your speeches.

Headings:

Title:
General Purpose:
Specific Purpose:
Central Idea:

I. *Introduction*

    A. Gain attention.

    B. Relate to the audience.

    C. Establish your credibility.

    D. Preview your main points.

II. *Body*

    A. Main point

        1. Supporting material

            a. Specific information (such as a statistic)

            b. Specific information (such as a quotation)

        2. Supporting material

    B. Main point

        1. Supporting material

        2. Supporting material

            a. Specific information (such as a statistic)

            b. Specific information (such as a quotation)

                1) Very specific information for this subpoint

                2) Additional very specific information

III. *Conclusion*

    A. Signal the end.

    B. Review your main points.

    C. Tie to the introduction.

    D. End with impact.

Bibliography:

Include three or more sources, depending on the assignment.
Use the proper citation information found on page 156 in the text.

10

Audiovisual Resources

EVALUATING VISUALS

Evaluate the following visuals using the information contained in Chapter 10.

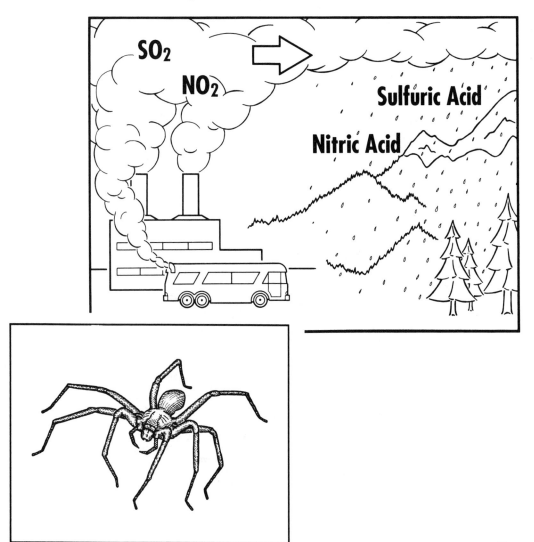

THE ART OF HITTING

1) CONCENTRATION

2) RELAXATION

3) BODY BALANCE

4) SEEING THE BALL

5) WEIGHT SHIFT

6) THROWING HIPS & SHOULDERS

7) THROWING HANDS

8) FOLLOW THROUGH

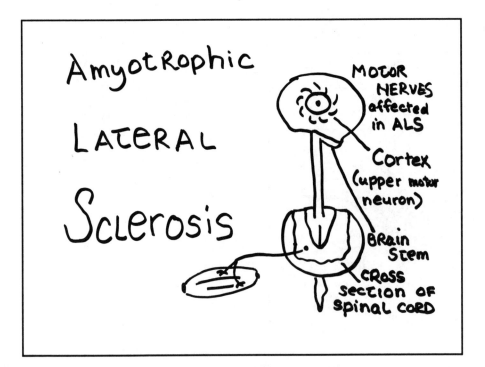

Amyotrophic

LATERAL

Sclerosis

MOTOR NERVES affected in ALS

Cortex (upper motor neuron)

Brain Stem

CROSS Section OF Spinal coRD

━━━━━━

SPEECH ASSIGNMENT:
Audiovisual Aid Speech

Time: 5–6 minutes

Description

This is an informative speech that requires skillful use of audio or visual support.

Specific Skills

Fully developed introduction and conclusion
Clearly stated main points
Support for each main point
Use of signposts
Use of at least two research sources
Skillful use of audio or visual aids

Organizational Pattern

Chronological, spatial, or topical

Audiovisual Aids

Objects, charts, tape clips, graphs, drawings, and/or other audiovisual aids are required for this presentation. They should support, rather than substitute for, the main ideas of the speech.

Informative Options

Process. A speech clarifying a process by which something is done, is created, or occurs. You may actually demonstrate the process. (See pages 323–325 in Chapter 14.) Topics should add to the knowledge of a college-level audience.

Examples: How the lottery system works; stages of grief; how to analyze handwriting; the progress of a disease; how to upgrade a computer; how to do calligraphy; the process of learning in senior adults.

Biography. A speech giving the main life events and accomplishments of a famous individual who has made significant contributions to society. (See pages 319–320.)

Examples: Choose subjects who contributed positively—or negatively—to society: Medgar Evars, Nostradamus, Anastasia. Supreme Court justices, politicians, artists, entertainers, military officers, musicians, and so on make good subjects. Think of subjects from other cultures and other times.

Explanation or Description. A speech that explains a complex idea or describes a place, event, or object—how it is made, how it works, its significance, and so on. (Pages 321–323, 326–327 give more detail.)

Examples: lucid dreaming, noninvasive medications, Norplant (a relatively new contraceptive), the Suez Canal, a wedding in another culture, a Romanian orphanage, an ostrich.

Reading: Chapter 9
Chapter 14

SPEECH OUTLINE: Process Speech

Topic:	How to fill out a 1040 IRS Form
General Purpose:	To inform
Specific Purpose:	To inform my audience about how to gather, report, and assess information on the 1040 form
Central Idea:	Obtaining data, disclosing information, and assessing the aftereffects of an IRS report are the three steps of filling out a 1040 IRS form.

[Before the speech, hand every student a copy of the 1040 form. In order to have them use it only at the appropriate time, staple a piece of blank paper over it.]

I. Introduction
    A. April 15—what does that date mean to you?
    B. Many people dread it as the deadline for filing tax returns.
        1. Everyone who receives a W-2 wage must file.
        2. Even children with accumulated interest on their bank accounts must file tax returns.
        3. You may be required to file now—and you most certainly will do so in the future; you will want to save money on the process.
    C. I am majoring in finance, and I learned through my courses and my experience that filing a return is not as hard as others make it seem.

D.   Today, I will show you how to fill out the 1040 form by collecting data, disclosing information, and assessing the aftereffects of the process.

[Display a list on a transparency previewing the three steps.]

II.   Body

A.   The first step, obtaining and assessing data, is probably the most difficult.

1.   The most important piece of information is the W-2 Wage Statement that your employer mails in January.

2.   The IRS also mails the 1040 form in a tax packet.

3.   Group all other receipts of income and expenses for the year into appropriate categories.

[Display a second transparency listing possible categories: medical expenses, charitable contributions, interest on loans, etc.]

a.   Save all this information and file it away for at least five years.

b.   Information reported on the 1040 form must have backup support in case of future audit.

B.   The second step is to disclose all relevant information on the 1040 form.

[Display a visual of a 1040 form that has been transferred to a transparency; also ask listeners to remove the cover sheet on their handouts.]

1.   Report all income in the income section—even trivial amounts.

2.   Add or multiply interest factors where applicable.

3.   Don't skip any lines; this may cause miscalculation.

4.   Be sure to sign your return; it is void with no signature.

C.   Finally, determine the aftereffects of your return.

1.   Were you completely truthful?

a.   Would your 1040 hold up during an audit?

b.   False information may lead to a fine, even imprisonment.

2.   If you expect a refund, it may take up to twelve weeks to get a check in the mail.

III.   Conclusion

A.   The 1040 is a standard form each American worker must file.

B.   It is simple enough that you can fill it out yourself.

[Review the three steps by displaying the first list again.]

C.   April 15—don't forget this date—it will never change.

D.   It's a date the IRS looks forward to!

References

H & R Block (1989). *H & R Block 1990 income tax guide.* New York: Macmillan Publishing.

Internal Revenue Service (1991). IRS Tax Preparation Booklet.

Sheth, S. (1991, October 18). Personal interview.

Adapted from an outline by Nila Sheth, St. John's University, 10/25/91

SPEECH OUTLINE:
Biographical Speech

Topic:	Hector Berlioz
General Purpose:	To inform
Specific Purpose:	To inform my audience about the Romantic composer, Hector Berlioz
Central Idea:	Hector Berlioz was a true romantic composer who introduced several important ideas into music composition.

  I. Introduction

[Play a 15-second clip of Berlioz's music during points A & B of the outline.]

     A. (Voice over, pausing between words) unearthly sounds . . . nighttime . . . distant horn calls . . . summoning . . .

     B. Most of us have experienced this haunting effect.

        1. Possibly we've read or heard a horror story—or we've heard this type of background music during a scary movie.

        2. Hector Berlioz was the musician who created such effects in music.

     C. As a musician trained in piano, clarinet, and guitar, I attended Fiorello H. LaGuardia of Music and Art High School, where I was required to study music history and research the lives of musicians and composers.

     D. I will share with you some aspects of Hector Berlioz's fascinating biography and explain the important contributions he made in music composition.

 II. Body

     A. To understand him, we must go back in time to the early nineteenth century, commonly remembered as the Romantic Period.

[Display drawing of Berlioz that has been transferred to a transparency.]

        1. He was born in 1803 into a well-to-do physician's family, and he grew up in a period when romantic poets and writers dominated literature.

a. As a child he read travel books and longed for adventures in faraway countries.

b. He learned flute and guitar, but never the piano.

c. He learned harmony from books without reference to a keyboard.

d. When he was 12, like a true romantic, he fell passionately in love with an 18-year-old who influenced his first compositions—at age 13.

2. When he was ready for university studies, his father sent him to Paris to study to be a doctor like himself.

a. Hector could not imagine dissecting rats—and human bodies.

b. Instead he decided to abandon medicine (and parental funds) and attend the Paris Conservatory of Music.

3. One night at the theater, he fell madly in love from afar with an actress named Harriet Smithson—and with Shakespearean plays.

a. According to rumor, he followed her theater group performances.

b. Eventually they married, but the reality of marriage did not match his romantic notions of it.

c. His passion for Shakespeare inspired major works on *Hamlet* and *The Tempest*.

B. His temperament led to musical innovations.

1. One is the *idée fixe*, or dominant theme, that recurs throughout a Berlioz symphony.

a. The idea of a dominant, recurring theme ties into Romanticism.

b. It is linked to his obsessive love for Harriet; he made her his *idée fixe* in one of his greatest symphonies, the Fantastic Symphony.

c. The composer varies theme by adjusting pace, pitch, meter, or orchestration.

d. This is the dominant theme that recurs throughout that symphony.

[Play short excerpt—then cut to a variation that appears later.]

2. Another innovation was the five-movement symphony—known as "grandiose"—instead of the usual four-movement compositions.

3. Berlioz also used instruments in imaginative ways; for example, plucking violins created the sound of flying bats.

[Play an excerpt that demonstrates this.]

   4. He was keenly aware of the importance of matching sound to
      space.

      a. He did not like large orchestras in small spaces.

      b. But in large spaces, he used orchestras of approximately 120
         people to create a massive sound, uncommon in his time.

[Play a short musical clip that illustrates this.]

III. Conclusion

   A. In conclusion, this true Romantic broke new ground with his original
      ideas, and he has inspired many composers.

   B. In his time, his massive orchestra was too awkward, the five movements
      made his symphonies long and boring, and his odd use of instruments
      for sound effects was unappreciated.

   C. However, he is appreciated today precisely for his eccentric innovations.

   D. And what is a horror movie without the music that evokes our fears?

References

Berlioz, H. (1975). *The memoirs of Hector Berlioz: Member of the French Institute including his travels in Italy, Germany, Russia, and England* (D. Cairn, Trans., Ed.).
   New York: W. W. Norton.

Berlioz, H. (1975). Symphonie Fantastique, Op. 14 [sound recording]. Berliner
   Philharmoniker. Herbert von Karajan (conductor). Deutsche Grammophon.

Holoman, D. K. (1989). *Berlioz.* Cambridge: Harvard University Press.

Kerman, J. (1987). *Listen: Brief edition.* New York: Worth Publishers.

Macdonald, H. (Ed.) (1980). Berlioz, (Louis) Hector. In S. Sadie, *The new Grove
   dictionary of music and musicians* (Vol. 2). Washington, DC: Grove.

(Speech by Yesenia Abreu, summer 1992, St. John's University)

SPEECH OUTLINE:
Explanatory Speech

Topic:	Dolphin communication
General Purpose:	To inform
Specific Purpose:	To inform my audience about the studies being conducted in the area of human–dolphin communication
Central Idea:	Researchers have taught dolphins to communicate through a series of whistles and object association.

I. Introduction

    A. "Hoop Right Frisbee In"; you may not understand this, but a dolphin trained to communicate with humans would know exactly what I meant.

    B. Language forms a barrier that prevents us from communicating with life outside our "human" world, but studies involving the bottlenose dolphin show that we are not the only intelligent animals on earth, and communication with some animals is possible.

    C. I first learned of the dolphin's ability to understand and communicate with humans when I read an article for a writing course; while researching the topic, I found several additional articles and books related to dolphin communication.

    D. I would like to explain the concept of dolphin intelligence, dolphin-to-dolphin communication, and dolphin communication with humans.

II. Body

    A. Many scientists think that dolphins have a very high intelligence level and, in this area, they may be the animal closest to a human.

        1. *Sea Frontiers Magazine* reports that dolphins have the highest ratio of brain-to-body size of any nonhuman animal; this ratio may indicate the ability to process large amounts of complex information.

        2. However, intelligence is not entirely based on brain size.

            a. It is also related to how information is processed and used.

                1) Quickness and efficiency are important.

                2) Flexibility, the ability to adapt to moment-by-moment happenings, is also important.

            b. Dolphins have proven that they can quickly, efficiently, and flexibly process information.

        3. Researchers have found that dolphins can mimic some human sounds.

            a. This indicates an ability to remember certain sounds.

            b. It also suggests they may be able to communicate in an artificial language.

    B. Dolphins communicate among themselves.

        1. According to *The Natural History of Whales and Dolphins*, they communicate through a system of whistles, clicks, rattles, and squeaks.

            a. Clicking sounds, which are used for navigation in deep waters, may also convey messages.

                1) Pulsed squeaks can indicate distress.

                2) Buzzing clicks may indicate aggression.

    2.   Dolphins identify themselves through signature whistles.

        a.   Each dolphin has a distinctive signature whistle it uses to identify itself to other dolphins.

        b.   Mothers and calves find each other in large groups, even when other dolphins are also whistling.

    3.   An article titled "Those Dolphins Aren't Just Whistling in the Dark" suggests that dolphins may even pass down legends or stories.

        a.   This idea seems a little far-fetched.

        b.   However, animals seem to understand things in their own way.

  C.   Through training, captive dolphins have learned to associate sounds with objects and actions.

    1.   In one study, researchers used an underwater keyboard.

[Display transparency showing the nine-key keyboard.]

        a.   Symbols on each of nine keys represented a specific type of object.

           1)   The symbol was not a picture of the object.

           2)   The keys could be moved around on the board so that the dolphins could not memorize the location.

[Display second transparency showing keys in a different position.]

        b.   When dolphins pressed a key, a distinctive whistle was sounded, and they received the object associated with the symbol on the key.

           1)   They soon learned to associate the symbol with the object.

           2)   Dolphins would give the "ball" whistle before pressing the key.

           3)   When they saw two items at once, such as a ring and a ball, they would make both whistles as they played with the objects.

        c.   They remembered these sounds on a long-term basis.

           1)   Researchers separated them from the keyboard for two years.

           2)   When they saw it again, they happily began to whistle the various sounds.

    2.   Dolphins could understand "sentences" that combined various objects or actions they learned to associate with whistles.

        a.   Each sentence was two to five words long.

      b. Sentences consisted of an indirect object, a direct object, and a term that connected them.

         1) For example, "HOOP RIGHT FRISBEE IN" meant, "Put the frisbee in the hoop on the right."

         2) Word order mattered; reversing the order in the sentence would result in a totally different response.

      c. Dolphins could understand a variety of word combinations.

         1) Once an instructor said "WATER TOSS," thinking this was a nonsense sentence that would get no response.

         2) The dolphin quickly moved to the hose on the tank's railing and glided through it, sending out a spray of water.

III. Conclusion

    A. In conclusion, we are not the only intelligent creatures on earth.

    B. Dolphins are intelligent animals who communicate with one another and with humans through an invented "language" of whistles and clicks.

    C. The next time you hear somebody talking to her dog as if it were a person, don't automatically assume that she is crazy; she may know something about communicating with animals that dolphin studies hint at.

References

Bower, B. (1984, December 1). Grammar-schooled dolphins. *Science News*, pp. 346–348.

Curtis, P. (1987, January/February). Contact with dolphins. *Sea Frontiers*, pp. 84–92.

Evans, P. G. H. (1987). *The natural history of whales and dolphins.* New York: Oxford.

Forcier-Beringer, A. C. (1986, March/April). Talking with dolphins. *Sea Frontiers*, pp. 84–92.

Sayigh, L. S., & Pyack, P. L. (1989, Spring). Those dolphins aren't just whistling in the dark. *Oceanus*, pp. 80–83.

Shane, S. H. (1991, March/April). The dolphin report. *Sea Frontiers*, pp. 36–43.

Wintsch, S. (1990, Fall). You'd think you were thinking. *Mosaic*, pp. 34–48.

Outline by Tanya Moser (1992, April 23). Oregon State University, Corvallis, OR. (Adapted)

██████████

EVALUATION FORM

Speech with Audiovisual Aid

Name_____ Time _____

Disposition

_____Attention gained
_____Related to audience
_____Credibility established
_____Previewed
_____Organization clear
_____Main points clear
_____Signaled conclusion
_____Tied to introduction
_____Summarized
_____Ended with impact

Invention

_____Topic of significance (need)
_____Informative purpose
_____Audience related
_____Speaker credibility demonstrated throughout
_____Adequate supporting material
_____Evidence of research
_____All details relevant
_____VISUAL AID

Style

_____Precision of language
     (NOT: "What you do is you . . ." "You want to . . .")

Delivery

_____Voice: rate, volume, variety, quality
_____Posture and gestures
_____Other: appearance and eye contact

Memory

_____Minimal use of note cards
_____Fluency of thought

                                                             Grade_____

11

Language

USE OF IMAGERY

Page 258 in the text states the importance of vivid language that helps listeners see, feel, and thus remember your speech. Imagery is figurative language that results in listeners imagining or creating mental images of what you are talking about.

You can use five basic types of images that appeal to the senses of:

1. Sight.
2. Hearing.
3. Smell.
4. Taste.
5. Touch.

The following examples come from student speeches. Underline the vivid images in each, then try to imagine how you would react if the speaker had used boring language.

Have you ever bitten into a fat, juicy, bacon double cheeseburger with onions, pickles, ketchup, and mayonnaise so that the juices just ooze out? At one time or another, most have probably eaten what I call a heart attack on a bun. (Andrés Lucero)

Peaceful and serene, quiet and cool, it's a day for fishing with your family. The sun is shining on your face, the wind blowing softly on your body, and there are no worries of work, traffic, or the bustle of city life. (Jill Nagaue)

It is common to see scientists jump into the arena of faith issues, make some absurd claim that everyone must believe in their conclusions because of their knowledge, and then nimbly hop back out of the arena where their colleagues clap them on the back and congratulate them on their brilliant deductions. (Jeffrey Grimes)

In my own part of Africa, the climate is wonderful and agreeable, but it never snows. Upon arriving in the United States during the fall, well-meaning persons overemphasized to me the gravity of a Michigan winter and its terrible snow. I thought that when it fell, it would come in thick, hard masses that would almost break my head if I didn't have shelter or protection! But now, having lived with snow for two years, we are friends, and I now fervently wish that we in Nigeria, while retaining our God-given beautiful sunshine, could have snow too! (Larry Fabunmi)

Gerard [Majella] had a weak, delicate appearance and seemed more of a ghost than a man. He was long and lanky and had an emaciated face. (Daniel Kelly)

WORSHEET:
Eliminating Clutter

This draft of a speech contains many unnecessary words. Working with a partner, eliminate unnecessary words. In some cases, you may have to reword the sentence slightly.

WHEN ONE MENTIONS THE WORD DESTINY, IT AUTOMATICALLY CONJURES UP A VISION OF SOMETHING BEYOND THE POWER OR CONTROL OF ORDINARY HUMANS. INDIVIDUALS HAVE OFTEN REFERRED TO DESTINY AS AN UNAVOIDABLE LOT, FATE, OR EVEN DOOM THAT HAS ALREADY BEEN PREDETERMINED BY SOME IR-RESISTIBLE POWER.

THE ROMANS USED TO HAVE A LATIN SAYING: *"DESTINATUM EST MINI,"* MEANING, "I HAVE MADE UP MY MIND." HERE, DES-TINY STOOD FOR AN ACT THAT WAS FIXED OR DETERMINED. LATER ON, WE SEE THE WORD REAPPEARING IN BOTH THE OLD AND MIDDLE FRENCH VOCABULARY IN THE FEMININE FORM *"DESTINE."* FINALLY, FROM THE MIDDLE ENGLISH WORD *"DESTINEE"* (WHICH WAS SPELLED WITH A DOUBLE "E" AT THE END), WE GET THE MODERN-DAY FORM OF THE WORD AS WE KNOW IT TODAY.

HOWEVER, IT ISN'T A WORD'S ETYMOLOGICAL HISTORY WE SEE WHEN WE READ OR USE A SPECIFIC WORD. MANY TIMES WE DON'T SEE OR FEEL ANYTHING AT ALL, BUT, IN CERTAIN IN-STANCES, WORDS TEND TO CARRY A DEEPER MEANING—EVEN IF IT IS JUST ONE SINGLE WORD, AS IS THE CASE WITH DESTINY.

SPEECH ASSIGNMENT:
Speech of Definition

Description

Words are symbols in the code called language that allows humans to communicate. Words as symbols have meaning only because a group of people agree that the symbols represent an object, thought, or feeling. Often we hear the phrase, "Meanings are in people, not in words." Even within the same cultural context, there are many variations in the meaning of a single word.

You may choose to define a word or term from another language. There may not be an exact equivalent or translation directly into American English.

Skills

Define an abstract term so that its meaning and your interpretation of that meaning become clear to your audience.

Clearly define the term in a well-organized manner based on careful and thoughtful analysis.

Guidelines: Content and Organization

Main Point I: This point will focus on the *denotation* of the term according to various reference books (i.e., thesaurus, common use, etymological dictionaries, etc.)

    A. One of your references must be the *Oxford English Dictionary* or any unabridged dictionary.

    B. You must select two of the following methods of defining a term.

        1. Synonym and antonym.

        2. Use and function.

        3. Etymology and historical example.

        4. Comparisons.

Main Point II: This point will focus on the *connotation* of the term according to your own life experience. Be as creative as you wish in clarifying the term. Here are some ideas:

    A. Explain what the term means to you based on a personal experience.

    B. Illustrate your interpretation using several different methods.

        1. Telling a story.

        2. Giving examples.

3. Referring to a person who exemplifies the term.
4. Relating it to a political, social, or moral issue.
5. Anything else you can think of that may give your audience greater insight into the meaning of the word.

C. Quote other people as to what the term means to them.

Source: Beth Von Till and her associates at San Jose State University developed this assignment.

SAMPLE SPEECH:
Destiny

The word DESTINY—it automatically conjures up a vision of something beyond the power or control of ordinary humans. Individuals have often thought of destiny as an unavoidable lot, fate, or even doom that has already been predetermined by some irresistible power.

The Romans had a saying, "*Destinatum est mini*," meaning, "I have made up my mind." In Rome, destiny meant a decision was fixed or determined. Later, the word reappeared in both Old and Middle French in the feminine form *destiné*. Finally, from the Middle English word *destinee*, we get the modern form of the word.

However, it isn't the word's etymological history that is meaningful to me. You see, destiny is a depressing reminder of a car accident that took place last February involving both my sister and my father—an accident that left my sister in a state of shock, my father with a number of broken ribs and internal bleeding, and the car a total loss.

There wasn't any other party to blame for our misfortune. My sister's hasty decision to make a left turn at a busy intersection led to the crash—as our car was sideswiped on the passenger side by an oncoming vehicle.

When she returned from the hospital she cried hysterically, blaming herself for all the suffering caused to my father. I too felt her pain and guilt after my mom announced that his recovery would be slow and painful. In the months following, my mother and I helped my father through his recovery. My sister, on the other hand, dealt with her guilt by avoiding my father as much as possible.

With my father temporarily out of work, our family had to make financial, physical, and mental sacrifices. My college plans were altered, as were other features in my personal life. Our whole family attempted to put the ordeal behind us and concentrate on the goals and plans we had before the accident. Unfortunately, we knew all too well that many of these plans would similarly be altered or put on hold.

In the following months, I felt cheated and wondered why this had happened to us. Here was a situation that was pushing our lives into new directions. I managed to find some comfort in a Chinese proverb my social studies teacher told our class when we were upset: "You cannot prevent the birds of sorrow from flying over your head, but you can prevent them from building nests in your hair." He was right.

Life is full of unforeseen and trying events that we don't ask for and we can't control. However, they are just roadblocks on our paths to destiny. They help make us stronger so that the next one is easier to overcome. What really counts is how we deal with the situation.

William Jennings Bryan said, "Destiny is not a matter of chance, it is a matter of choice. It is not a thing to be waited for, it is a thing to be achieved." By choosing to overcome any obstacles and by persevering against the odds, we will find our destiny.

Terez Czapp, St. John's University (New York)

EVALUATION FORM

Speech of Definition

Name_____

Word Selected_____

Invention and Disposition

___Strong opening statement

___Denotative definition

   ___Dictionary definition

   ___1st method of definition

   ___2nd method of definition

___Connotative definition

   ___Term related to speaker

   ___Interpretation clearly illustrated

___Memorable ending

Style

___Language appropriate

___Concise

___Interesting language

Delivery

___Eye contact

___Gestures

___Extemporaneous delivery

Memory

___Evidence of rehearsal

___Minimal use of note cards

Grade _____

12

Delivery

DELIVERY WORKSHEET

Watch a videotape of a speech with the sound turned off. You are forming an impression of the speaker, not through the words of the speech, but through her or his nonverbal communication. Jot down notes in response to these questions as you watch:

1. Does the speaker have a *physical feature* that causes you to respond to him or her in a stereotyped manner? If so, what is it?

2. Evaluate the speaker's *grooming*. In what ways does it enhance or detract from the impression you are getting of the speaker?

3. Assess the appropriateness of the speaker's *clothing and accessories* for the audience and the situation.

4. In what ways are the speaker's *gestures* effective? ineffective?

   What *emblems* (if any) do you notice?

   What *illustrators* do you observe?

   Any *adaptors*?

5. Evaluate the speaker's *eye contact*.

What, if any, suggestions would you give this speaker in order for her or him to create a more favorable impression on you through nonverbal channels?

SPEECH ASSIGNMENT:
Audiotaped Speech

Description

You will audiotape a speech. Because taped speeches—such as radio commentaries—often occur within exact time limits, your instructor may ask you to time the speech to be exactly 1, 2, or 3 minutes in length.

Example: Terez Czapp audiotaped the speech "Destiny" (pp. 76–77).

Skills

Effective use of vocal variety
Manuscript delivery, read in a conversational manner
(opt.) Exact timing

Guidelines

1. Choose an assignment in this Student Resource Workbook or from Chapter 17 in the text. A tribute, speech of definition, exemplum, farewell, announcement, nomination, introduction, or goodwill speech works well. Prepare the speech, following the pattern and guidelines given in the workbook or text.

2. Since you cannot keep attention by visual means, organize your speech carefully to enable your listeners to identify your main points and remember them easily. Pay special attention to transitions, internal previews, and summaries to help listeners connect the points of the speech easily.

3. Write the script of the speech using capital letters and triple spacing.

4. (Opt.) Edit your material so that it is exactly one *or* two *or* three minutes in length.

5. You must convey shades of meaning through vocal variation alone. Pay special attention to pauses, accents, rate, and volume to enhance your message. Then mark your script accordingly.

   - For example, circle or use a colored highlighter on the words you plan to stress.
   - Put // (slash) marks where you intend to pause.
   - Put a ↑ where you want your tone to rise and a ↓ where you want it to fall.

6. Practice reading the script until you are satisfied that your delivery sounds conversational. Speak as if you were conversing with only one person. Mentally visualize a typical listener, then speak directly to that individual.

7. Taperecord your speech. Replay the tape, listening carefully to your voice. If you don't like what you hear, simply rerecord the speech until you are satisfied.

8. Bring the tape to class, cued up to the beginning of your final version.

EVALUATION FORM

Audiotaped Speech

Name_____ Time _____

Invention

____ Appropriate topic

____ Purpose clear

____ Main ideas clear

____ Main ideas supported

Disposition

____ Organizational pattern clear

____ Transitions, internal previews, and summaries

____ Effective introduction

____ Strong conclusion

Style

____ Language appropriate, clear

____ Interesting language

Delivery

____ Appropriate rate

____Volume

____Vocal variety

____ Effective use of pauses

____ Conversational delivery

Grade ____

AUDIOVISUAL MESSAGES

Speaking on film may be important in your future—for instance, you may participate in a video conference or be interviewed by a news reporter. Even if this seems remote now, more and more experts in one area or another are learning how to communicate effectively through filmed messages. They include politicians, doctors, educators, special interest advocates, pastors, and volunteer workers.

The simplest kind of filmed speech is taped by only one other person, the camera operator. The camera can be a portable hand-held camcorder operated by a nonprofessional. Or, it can be a fixed camera in a small studio that uses only one camera angle. Your school may have this equipment. Generally, you only film the speech once; however, if you make a major mistake, you can refilm the entire speech.

Other filmed presentations are highly sophisticated, requiring the assistance of a variety of professionals including producers, stage managers, lighting directors, makeup artists, directors, and editors. This team works together to create a polished presentation.

Making a filmed presentation differs from other speaking in a number of ways, and here are some tips for making videotaped messages.

1. Film is a close-up medium. Because of this, you need to appear honest and sincere, conveying your feelings and your personality as well as your ideas. Since the camera can zero in on your face by using extreme close-up (ECU) shots, control your facial expressions.

2. Similarly, control your bodily movement and posture. Eliminate sweeping gestures, walking, scratching, nervous mannerisms, and other motions that are not essential to convey your ideas. Work to be graceful and fluid in the movements you do use. Relax so that you appear comfortable.

3. Wardrobe consultants suggest these clothing tips:
   - Blue or gray tones photograph better than solid black or white.
   - Avoid "busy" patterns and very small plaids or stripes.
   - Men should choose off-white or pastel shirts and simple ties.
   - Keep jewelry to a minimum—and then, wear only simple pieces.
   - Avoid shiny, highly reflective fabrics.

4. When using a TelePrompTer, rehearse in advance with a technician. Have him or her adjust the speed of the lines to your speaking rate and circle or underline key words or phrases. Practice for a conversational delivery.

Although you may think this type of speaking is not in your future, learning to use technology effectively will almost certainly enhance your career.

See E. L. Hilliard (Ed.) (1978), *Television broadcasting: An introduction*. New York: Hasting House; and B. Shanks (1976), *The cool fire: How to make it in television*. New York: W. W. Norton.

SPEECH ASSIGNMENT:
Thirty-Second Videotaped Speech

Description

Prepare and videotape a thirty-second speech.

Skills

Choose an appropriate speech purpose—to convince, reinforce, inform, or actuate your audience.
Deliver a speech effectively using cue cards or a TelePrompTer.
Use nonverbal skills to deliver your speech effectively on camera.
Edit your material to fit precisely into a time frame.

Guidelines

1. Choose a single idea that you can convey in a short period of time.

    Examples of TV editorials:

    *   A woman who had adopted racially mixed children told the audience that she is happy to discuss adoption, but urged them not to ask, "Where did you get your children?" in the child's presence.

    *   A man urged people not to purchase a book by a convicted murderer. He contended that people should not become rich because of their crimes.

    Examples of student topics:

    *   One announced a community cleanup day and urged the audience to participate in it.

    *   One reinforced the cultural value of reaching out to others by urging listeners to donate to the food bank.

    *   One student rhymed his speech urging the audience to put on shorts and enjoy the last few days of autumn.

2. Organize your ideas. The single point speech found on pages 16–17, a simplified Monroe's Motivated Sequence (pages 393–396 in the text), or one of

the speeches found in Chapter 17—such as an announcement or nomination—are appropriate patterns.

3. Edit your speech so that it is exactly thirty seconds long. If a TelePrompTer is available, transfer the script to it. If not, write it onto large cue cards that you read during the videotaping as someone holds them near the camera.

4. Videotape your speech, using the cue cards or a TelePrompTer.

5. After you view all the speeches in the class, discuss the following questions:

    1. What was the easiest part of this assignment? What was most difficult?

    2. What topics, if any, did you consider and discard as possibilities? Why?

    3. What can be "covered" in thirty seconds? What cannot?

SAMPLE THIRTY-SECOND SPEECH: Tinnitis

Patrick Barbo, whose outline on tinnitus appears in the text, modified his speech for a thirty-second televised speech.

YOU ONLY HAVE TWO HANDS, AND I BET YOU DON'T TAKE A HAMMER AND SLAM THOSE HANDS EVERY DAY AND EXPECT THEM TO WORK PROPERLY.

BUT YOU ONLY HAVE TWO EARS AND YET MOST PEOPLE SLAM THEM EVERYDAY WITH LOUD NOISE WITHOUT EVEN THINKING TWICE ABOUT DAMAGE BEING DONE.

REDUCING THE VOLUME OF YOUR RADIO OR STEREO WOULD PREVENT DAMAGING YOUR HEARING.

FIRST IMAGINE WHISTLES INSIDE YOUR HEAD IF YOU DESTROY YOUR EARS, THEN IMAGINE A LIFE WITHOUT HEARING PROBLEMS.

YOU CHOOSE. IT'S UP TO YOU. KEEP THE VOLUME DOWN.

EVALUATION FORM

Thirty-Second Speech

Name_____ Time _____

Invention and Disposition

____ Topic appropriate to the time limit

____ Purpose clear

____ Major idea clear

____ Supporting material to the point

____ Organized well

____ Edited well

Style

____ Language appropriate, clear

____ Interesting languge

Delivery

____ Timing

____ Pleasant facial expressions

____ Appropriate gestures

____ Camera-appropriate clothing

____ Camera-appropriate grooming

____ Vocal variety

____ Appropriate speaking rate

____ Volume

____ Conversational-sounding delivery

Grade____

UNIT III

Applied Contexts

13

Narrative Speaking

SPEECH ASSIGNMENT:
Narrative Speech

Time: 3–5 minutes

Description

The purpose of this assignment is to tell a story that reinforces an important cultural resource. This may be a belief, a value, an attitude, or an action. A humorous story may present your point effectively.

Skills

Identify an important cultural resource: belief, value, attitude, action.
Use a story or example that illustrates that resource.
Begin with impact.
Choose a pattern that effectively organizes the main points.
Edit to achieve economy, unity, definiteness of characterization.
Choose a narrative that passes the tests for narrative merit.
Test the reasonableness of your narrative.
End with impact.

Guidelines for Narrative

1. Choose a narrative function—that is, decide if you want to explain a belief, to provide an example, to persuade your audience, or to offer possibilities that are yet unrealized. Remember that reinforcing a value—as is done in an exemplum—is a form of persuasion.

2. Identify the characters. What personality characteristics do they have? How do they look? speak? act?

3. Plot—what happens in the story? What crisis or crises do the characters face?

4. Identify the theme or major idea their story conveys.

5. Select an organizational pattern that meets your needs. Choose from the spiral pattern (found in the text, pages 190–191), the infinity loop pattern (pages 306–308), or the exemplum pattern (found on pages 308–309 in the text). In some speeches, the chronological pattern may be most appropriate.

6. Polish the language in the speech. Select vivid, descriptive words. Include more details at the beginning and at points of conflict. Use lists and dialogue where appropriate.

Reading review: Chapters 9 and 13

SAMPLE NARRATIVE:
Lee Johnson's Revenge

It might, like many another racial incident, have left the community and the victim embittered.

J. Lee Johnson, 34, a black entrepreneur in Lawrence, New Jersey, arrived at his computer company to find racial slurs painted on the walls and a dead bird lying on the doorstep. He had just opened a new company in the neighborhood.

The graffiti contained references to the KKK, a drawing of a painted cross, and a slur that read, "No Nigir." As the local paper wrote, "The green spray-painted words were crude and one was even misspelled, but their meaning was clear: blacks are not welcome."

Johnson, whose parents were raised in the South and who knew firsthand the racism they had undergone, did not feel welcome. "At first I didn't know what to do," he says. "This was like a cold slap in the face. It knocked a little bit of the wind out of my sails."

But Johnson is tough. His parents had also brought him up never to hate anyone because of their race or religion. "Most people thought I would be in a retaliatory mood," he told me. "But we can't afford to let these things rip our communities."

Local residents and businesspeople rallied round, telling him what had happened was deplorable and didn't reflect the feeling in the neighborhood. "They told me to hang in there." The mayor came by, expressing her horror and the commitment of the community that such actions would not be tolerated. Churches and other community groups, aware that racial incidents, although uncommon, were not unknown in the area, set up support networks. Johnson's mailbag was "stuffed" with letters from caring people.

Five days after the incident the police had charged the vandal—a ten-year-old boy. "I was floored," Johnson told a racist sensitivity training session at the local Episcopal church. "You really can't say it's the parents' fault. Kids are exposed to hatred and violence on television every day. It's what we are as a community. It's coming out in small children, and it's got to stop."

He decided to reach out to the young man as others had done to him earlier in life, believing that America cannot afford to lose a generation to hatred and bias.

The white youngster had never met a black man. Johnson gave him a tour of his business, meeting blacks, whites, and Hispanics working there. He introduced him to the inside of computers. They sat and talked on the very spot where the boy had left the dead bird.

Today, Johnson says, the boy is doing better at home and school. "He has found a place to channel energies that had gone astray. I like to visualize ten years down the road, what would be his mindset if we don't reach out and show him the beauty of differences in people."

The blotches of paint on the wall that cover over the graffiti still remain. Johnson can't yet afford to paint the building. They are a constant reminder of the past. But the friendship he has built with a young boy who knew no better is a stake in a different future and part of the cure to what he calls the threatening disease of prejudice. A community is the richer for his action.

Michael Henderson, a native of England who lives in the Northwest, gave this commentary over KBOO radio station in Portland, Oregon.

EVALUATION FORM

Narrative Speech (Exemplum Pattern)

Name_____ Time _____

Exemplum Pattern

_____Quotation clearly stated

_____Source identified and described adequately

_____Quotation paraphrased

_____Narrative that illustrates it

_____Application to the audience

Cultural Value

_____Clearly identified

_____Relevant to this audience

_____Demonstrated in the narrative

Editing

_____All points relevant?

_____Characters clearly defined

_____Unity of speech

Language

_____Constructed dialogue (if appropriate)

_____Effective placement of details

Delivery

_____Minimal use of note cards

_____Direct eye contact

_____Posture and gestures appropriate

_____Conversational

_____Fluency of thought

Grade_____

━━━━━━

EVALUATION FORM

Narrative Speech (Alternative Pattern)

Name_____ Time _____

Invention

____Purpose is clear

____Story characters clearly defined

____Plot developed—climax, change in characters

____Adequate development throughout

____Narrative merit (story is worth telling)

Cultural Significance

____Point of story reveals significant cultural value, attitude, behavior, or belief

____Relevant to this audience

____Demonstrated in the narrative

Disposition

____Effective conclusion

____Organizational pattern clear

____Effective introduction

____Parts of speech effectively connected

Language

____Constructed dialogue (if appropriate)

____Effective placement of details

____Listing (where appropriate)

Delivery

____Minimal use of note cards

____Direct eye contact

____Posture and gestures appropriate

____Conversational

____Fluency of thought

Grade____

14

Informative Speaking

INFORMATIVE PURPOSES

The general goal of informative speaking is to add to your listeners' knowledge and, thus, their understanding of a subject. As the text points out, it is important to assess what your audience already knows and believes about your subject.

- Some audiences have never even heard of your topic.
- Others have limited knowledge.
- Still others have forgotten some or most of what they once knew.
- Finally, some have misconceptions and misunderstandings.

Consequently, after you have analyzed your audience's knowledge, narrow the general purpose "to inform" to correspond to your listeners' knowledge about the subject, and prepare a speech to produce, to reinforce, or to clarify their understanding of your topic.

To Produce Understanding

When an audience knows little or nothing about a topic, your informative intention is to produce knowledge or understanding where there was none before. This is sometimes known as *initiating* knowledge because you provide your listeners with their initial encounter with the subject.

Examples:

Instructors speak to produce knowledge about public speaking to students who generally have never heard of the five canons of rhetoric.

Students choose topics such as lucid dreaming, tinnitus, Bishop Barbara Harris, and other people, processes, concepts, and objects that are unknown or only vaguely familiar to their audiences.

Specific Strategies for Producing Knowledge. Provide basic information and a general overview at this level. Define basic words and explain concepts carefully. Compare and contrast the lesser-known topic with something that is similar but more familiar.

For instance, define lucid dreaming, give an example that helps explain it, then compare and contrast it to the kind of dreaming that is more familiar to the audience. Sketch the major events of Barbara Harris's life, and capture one or two of her most important personal characteristics.

At other times, audiences members lack detailed, in-depth understanding of the subject. You hope to *increase* their knowledge by going beyond introductory-level facts and definitions.

Examples:

In introductory classes a professor may devote one lecture to the five canons; in advanced classes, the same professor may spend one or two weeks elaborating on each canon.

Students provide in-depth information on familiar topics such as savings accounts, the muppets, good nutrition, and stress.

Specific Strategies for Increasing Listeners' Understanding. Probe beneath the surface to discover details that are less commonly known. Then, add in-depth descriptions and explanations to what is already familiar. Provide little-known information about just one aspect of the topic.

Most people, for instance, learned in elementary school that they should select foods from a variety of food groups; don't repeat that information. Instead, present details about a single aspect of nutrition such as antioxidants. Tell what they are, why they are important, and how they function.

To Reinforce Knowledge

Since humans tend to forget what they once learned unless they review it occasionally, sometimes your informative aim is *to reinforce* or *to maintain* your audience's knowledge. For this reason, across the land thousands of people take refresher courses to review what they already know.

Examples:

Professors often review course material before an exam to help their students remember definitions and explanations of specific concepts and theories.

Student speakers who choose topics such as drinking and driving, seatbelts, or the importance of exercise face a special challenge. While they want to strengthen their listeners' understanding, they do not want to bore them by overexplaining commonly known facts.

Specific Strategies for Reinforcing Knowledge. The key is to present information in a creative way. Plan interesting, vivid illustrations and other supporting material, such as comparison and contrast, to help listeners conceptualize the subject from different perspectives. When appropriate, use humor, and otherwise strive to make the review fun.

To Clarify Understanding

Sometimes audience members think that they understand your topic, but they have their facts wrong. Your aim here is to *repair* knowledge, as it were, by clearing up conceptual misunderstandings and clarifying the concepts. Sometimes these misunderstandings are in the form of stereotypes and prejudices that often have accompanying emotions, usually negative, that can result in inappropriate behaviors. Thus, you must provide accurate information and deal with the emotional component surrounding the misconception.

Examples:

After an exam it may be clear that a number of students have confused the canons of style and delivery, so the professor again clarifies the distinction between those two canons.

Arab students in the United States often speak about Arab customs and concerns in an attempt to clear up prejudices that stem partly from distorted images in the American media.

Other students try to clear up misconceptions and counter myths about killer bees, sharks, pit bulls, U. S. history, myths surrounding a disease, and other similar topics that are widely misunderstood.

Specific Strategies for Clarifying Understanding. Present the best factual material you can find. When appropriate, use information discovered as a result of scientific studies, using quantification when it is available. Define terminology carefully, perhaps explaining the origin of words. Compare and contrast your topic with what listeners already know. In the case of stereotypes and prejudices, present positive aspects of the topic.

■■■■■■

SPEECH ASSIGNMENT:
Current Issue Speech (Informative)

Time: 6–7 minutes

Definition

Think of this speech as an investigative news report. Select a *current* problem or controversial topic and present it in a strictly objective manner. Visual aids may accompany this speech in a supporting role.

Consult at least three sources for this speech—one from within the last six months. During the discussion that follows your speech, be prepared to discuss any source you cite or list on your bibliography.

Specific Skills

Informative purpose

Inventional skills: use of example, statistics, testimony, audience analysis, speaker credibility, cited sources from library research

Disposition: use of transition statements, internal preview/internal summary; all organizational skills from the audiovisual speech

Style: language that is accurate, appropriate, clear, and interesting

Delivery: extemporaneous delivery from a key word outline

Guidelines

1. *Invention.* Topic choice sometimes causes stress. Select a subject that doesn't bore you to sleep, but one that does not make you so angry you cannot present an informative speech. Because of the nature of the assignment, you will probably not be an "expert."

   a. Present information that is not widely known. Most people know all they care to about abortion and other common controversial topics.

   b. Do research using *current* oral, print, or electronic materials. Define the problem. Identify its components. Gather statistics, examples, and testimony to support your main points.

2. *Disposition.* Select an organizational pattern that will help the audience get the most from your speech. Pro–con is often effective.

   a. Write your introduction. Gain attention and reveal your topic. Relate to the audience. Provide your qualifications for this topic. Preview your main points.

   b. Write your conclusion. Signal the end is near. Review main points. Refer to the introduction. Provide a memorable ending.

   c. Polish the speech by writing transition statements, internal summaries, and/or internal previews.

   d. Outline the speech, writing rhetorical labels in the margin. Type and proofread your work.

3. *Style.* Evaluate word choices and word combinations. Choose vivid words. Check pronunciation of words of which you are unsure.

4. *Memory and Delivery.* Put speaking outline on note cards. Write single cue words only—no complete sentences. Practice the speech. Time yourself. Edit.

Reading Review: Chapters 2, 14, 7, 8, and 9.

SAMPLE OUTLINE:
Current Issue Speech

Topic: Fetal-Cell Transplantation
General Purpose: To inform
Specific Purpose: To inform my audience about the positions taken by sup-
                    porters and opponents of fetal cell transplantation
Central Idea: The debate over fetal-cell transplantion s growing, and the
                    question of whether it is right or wrong remains.

Organizational Pattern: Pro–Con

I. *Introduction*

   A. In 1988, fetal brain cells were implanted deep into the brain of a fifty-two-year-old Parkinson's victim.

      1. Parkinson's, a progressive neurological disorder in which muscular control is reduced, affects 500,000 Americans a year.

      2. Traditional treatments all failed this man.

      3. Now he reports his voice is much stronger, his mind is sharper, and he can walk without cane or crutches.

   B. Miracle or menace? The debate over whether fetal tissue and cells should be transplanted into persons with crippling illnesses is growing.

   C. I first became aware of this topic through an article in *Time Magazine* about a couple who conceived a child in order to obtain fetal cells for their older daughter who had leukemia.

   D. I would now like to explain both sides of this controversy and how the public views it.

II. *Body*

   A. There are many supporters of fetal tissue transplantation.

      1. Supporters want research to continue.

         a. Fetal tissue is a promising tool because it is much less likely to be rejected by the recipient's immune system.

         b. While adult donors are in short supply, fetal tissue can be obtained from over one million abortions in the United States each year.

         c. Dr. Kevin Lafferty at the University of Colorado says, "The termination of pregnancy is legal in this country. The result is that there is fetal tissue available, which can either be discarded or used" (Kolata, 1990, p. 175).

         d. To Dr. Lafferty there is no question whether it should be used.

2. Supporters believe that the fetus is essentially a cadaver.

   a. They feel this cadaver should be used to develop more effec-
       tive methods of treating debilitating diseases.

      1) This justification says that adult cadavers are used in re-
          search.

      2) Why shouldn't fetal cadavers be used the same way?

   b. John Robertson, a law professor at the University of Texas, says
       that the dead fetus is essentially an organ donor whose cells
       should be used to treat horrible diseases (Simons, 1990).

3. Many supporters say it is all right to conceive (and abort if neces-
    sary) a child to give another family member a better chance of life.

   a. Norman Frost, a pediatrician and ethicist at the University of
       Wisconsin says, if you believe a woman is entitled to terminate
       a pregnancy for any reason, why is it any worse to terminate
       for this reason (Morrow, 1991)?

   b. Parents want babies for many reasons—reasons frivolous, prac-
       tical, emotional, or sentimental.

      1) Families need children to work the fields.

      2) In much of the world, children are social security for old
          age.

   c. Says Dr. Rudolf Brutow, "Does it make sense to conceive a
       child so that little Johnny can have a sister, while it is not ac-
       ceptable to conceive the same child so that Johnny can live?"

B. Just as there are voices arguing for fetal cell transplantation, an equally
    vocal group argues against it.

1. Some critics believe that if fetal transplants are perfected, this will
    lead to an industry of abortion for profit; they want the research
    stopped.

   a. John Willke, M.D., president of the National Right to Life
       Committee, says, "Certain types of research are unethical, no
       matter how useful the results" (Kolata, 1990, p. 175).

   b. He and others also say that this kind of research lends respect-
       ability to the practice of abortion.

2. The critics of fetal tissue research and transplantation believe that
    the fetus is essentially a victim.

   a. Their answer to the question, "Should we do harm so that
       good may come?" is, "No."

   b. In his argument against conception and abortion for fetal tis-
       sues, Arthur Caplan, Director of the Center for Biomedical

Ethics at the University of Minnesota, says, "Society will not tolerate killing one life for another" (Simons, 1990, p. 27).

3. Some critics argue that continuing research would result in a higher abortion rate.

   a. If a doctor told a woman that having an abortion would aid research, then this might give her another reason to have an abortion.

   b. Janice Raymond, a professor of Women's Studies and Medical Ethics at the University of Massachusetts, believes that the demand for fetal tissues will become so great that the supply from elective abortions will not fill the need.

      1) She fears women will be persuaded more and more by ill family members and by promises of payment to get pregnant in order to have abortions resulting in tissue for donation (Kolata, 1990).

      2) Simply put, the ends do not justify the means.

C. We have seen the arguments for and against fetal tissue; now let's look at the results of a survey conducted by *Time Magazine* in June of this year (Morrow, 1991).

[Display a transparency showing the results of this survey. Uncover each question and the percentages as they are discussed.]

Is it morally acceptable to:	YES	NO
a. Use fetal tissue to treat diseases?	36%	47%
b. Conceive and intentionally abort so the tissue can be used?	18%	71%
c. Abort the fetus if the tissue is not compatible for a transplant?	11%	89%
d. Conceive a child in order to obtain an organ or tissue to save the life of another child in the family?	47%	37%

If you or a close relative had a fatal disease that could possibly be cured by a transplant, which of these would you be willing to do?

	TOTAL
a. Purchase an organ or tissue?	56%
b. Conceive a child to provide the necessary organ or tissue?	24%
c. Apply emotional pressure to a relative to donate?	15%
d. Take legal action to force a relative to donate?	6%

III.   *Conclusion*

    A.   I hope my speech has shed some light on a rather controversial subject.

    B.   The issue of fetal tissue transplants poses some sharp ethical questions, but also seems to hold some exciting promise;

        1.   Both sides claim they want to save lives.

        2.   The issues will require time and experience to explore.

    C.   Miracle or menace? What do you think?

References

Kolata, G. (1990, December). Miracle or Menace? *Redbook,* pp. 174–176, 216.

Morrow, L. (1991, June 17). When One Body Can Save Another. *Time*, pp. 54–58.

Simons, A. (1990, November 19). Brave New Harvest. *Christianity Today*, pp. 24–28.

Adapted from a speech by Chris Patti, given in 1991. Used by permission.

██████

EVALUATION FORM

Current Issue Speech

Name_____ Time _____

_____Topic choice (significant)
_____Informative purpose

Disposition

_____Attention gained
_____Related to audience
_____Established credibility
_____Previewed
_____Organization clear
_____Main points clear
_____Main points supported
_____Transition/internal summary/preview
_____Signaled speech conclusion
_____Tied to intro
_____Review of main points
_____Ended memorably

Invention

_____Adequacy of support
_____Statistics
_____Example
_____Testimony
_____Relevant data
_____Cited sources

Style

_____Precise language
_____Vivid style

Memory

_____Evidence of practice

_____Fluency of thought

_____Minimal use of notes

Delivery

_____Voice: rate, pitch variation, volume, pauses

_____Eye contact

_____Posture

_____Gestures

Grade_____

15

Reasoning

Here are additional examples of the various kinds of reasoning; using the tests given in the text, evaluate the reasoning in each example.

Causal Reasoning

The newscaster Paul Harvey told of a group of women in one country who marched in protest of their treatment by the men in their society. It seems that these men insisted that the young women start wearing longer skirts because there was a drought in the country. Consequently, shorter skirts and a shortage of rain existed at the same time. The men believed that the length of women's skirts influenced the rainfall—short skirts meant a shortage of rain; longer skirts correlated to longer periods of rainfall.

Faulty causal reasoning can be easily seen when we look at this example from another culture. Think, however, of how other global citizens perceive some of our causal assumptions. For example, how might the Iraqi government explain the cause of the Gulf War, as compared to the U.S. government's explanation? (If the Iraqis see Kuwait as historically part of their country, how might they explain what the Americans saw as an "invasion" and a "takeover"?)

Dr. Helen Caldecott, an environmental activist, argued that nuclear energy produces scores of anencephalic births (babies born with no brain, only a brain stem) in towns along the U.S.–Mexican border. She told one audience, "Every time you turn on an electric light, you are making another brainless baby."

(Facts: The incidence of anencephalic birth has risen in Mexican border towns; so has the incidence of other types of toxic waste dumping and environmental pollution.)

Parallel Case Reasoning

Not only do we use an actual case to formulate policies, when employing parallel case reasoning, we also make predictions about the future, based on the past.

Thus, we predict that what happened in a known case will happen in a similar case that we project, reasoning like this: "The policy worked (or didn't work) in this case that we know; thus, it will work (or will not work) in this similar case we are proposing." For example, after the 1993 federal budget passed through Congress, one senator who voted against the package used this argument to explain his opposition to the legislation:

> It didn't work when Congress passed a similar measure in 1990. A similar policy did not work when California tried it. It did not work in New Jersey. It will not work now.

Inductive Reasoning

Kathi reasons that American-made cars are no good. She purchased one and had a lot of trouble with it—first one thing went, then another. During a two-year period, she put over $1000 in repairs in the car.

How might she find out if her car is typical of others of the same model and make? Or is hers an isolated case?

How might the age of the car make a difference?

Deductive Reasoning

Early in the fight against AIDS, people thought the disease might be passed by such contact as sharing drinking glasses with infected persons. However, that premise was proven untrue by scientists who studied modes of transmission for the disease. The commonly accepted premise is now, "People who exchange body fluids with HIV positive individuals are at risk for AIDS."

One student argued that the conclusion, "We are all at risk for AIDS," does not follow from this premise. He offered instead a different syllogism, like this:

(Major premise): People who do not exchange body fluids with HIV positive individuals are not at risk for AIDS.

(Minor premise): You do not exchange body fluids with HIV positive individuals.

(Conclusion): Therefore, you are not at risk for AIDS.

16

Persuasive Speaking

SPEECH ASSIGNMENT:
Speech to Persuade

6–7 minutes

Definition

The purpose of this speech is to alter or reinforce attitudes, values, beliefs, or actions.

Specific Skills

All previous skills of invention and disposition
All previous skills of style and delivery
Use of proofs: audience (pathos), speaker (ethos), and rational (logos)

Guidelines

1. Select a topic, using the suggestions found on pages 378–379 of the text. What do you believe or feel strongly about? What will create a better society or better, more fulfilled individuals?

2. Decide on a claim of fact, value, or policy.

3. Analyze your audience's current beliefs and behaviors, attitudes, and values as they relate to your topic.

4. Plan how you will intertwine appeals to logic, to emotion, and to your credibility in order to be more persuasive.

5. Choose an organizational pattern that is appropriate for the subject matter and purpose of your speech. Prepare an introduction, conclusion, and connectives that make your speech "flow."

6. Pay attention to language choices, checking for clarity, accuracy, and interest.

7. Outline the contents of your speech. Type your outline. Make a speaking outline on note cards using key words only.

8. Rehearse.

Examples

To actuate behavior—The average American's junk mail adds up to 1½ trees' worth of paper annually; save trees by writing and having your name removed from junk mail lists.

To convince of a policy—Because Americans need to conserve fossil fuels, and because cars get better gas mileage at slower speeds, the nation should return to the 55 mph speed limit.

To convince of a value—Educational choice is good because it allows people to have personal control over their lives.

To reinforce a belief or value—Democracy continues to be the best system of government in the world today.

Reading Review: Chapters 15 and 16

SAMPLE OUTLINE:
Speech to Persuade (to Convince)

Topic:	Japan Bashing
General Purpose:	To inform
Specific Purpose:	To inform my audience about Japan bashing and its repercussions
Central Idea:	It appears that Japan bashing is widely accepted in the United States, but there are effects that people do not realize.

Organizational Pattern: Problem–Effects

I. *Introduction*

   A. Not long ago we thought of Japanese products as inferior and of poor quality.

   B. When you think of Japan today, what do you think of? Ninjas? Sushi bars? Sonys? Toyotas?

      1. You probably do not consider Japanese products inferior; in fact, Japan has become a great economic power.

      2. But there is a dark side to this success, stemming from economic frustration and possibly envy—Japan bashing.

   C. About a month ago I watched two Oprah Winfrey shows dealing with Japan bashing, and as an American of Asian descent, I decided to do further research.

       1. On one, Americans of Asian descent discussed their experiences due to fallout from Japan bashing.

       2. On the other, a panel made up of protectionists and American businesspeople who opposed protectionist policies debated the issue.

   D. Today, I will show what Japan bashing is and discuss its impact, both economically and racially, on our own society.

II. *Body*

   A. First, let's look at the problem of Japan bashing.

       1. Prominent, respected Americans make bashing statements.

          a. Former Treasury Secretary John Connally said, "They'd better be prepared to sit on the docks of Yokohama in their Toyotas watching their Sony sets, because they aren't going to ship them here" (Shapiro, 1992, p. 23).

          b. Senator Tom Harkin, a presidential candidate in 1992, said, "We're going to reduce our trade deficit with you, Japan, down to zero in five years. Two ways you can do it: buy more or sell us less" (Shapiro, 1992, p. 23).

          c. Michigan House Representative John Dingell added, "American jobs were being lost to little yellow men" (Wu, 1992, p. 11).

          d. President George Bush made jokes about throwing up on the prime minister of Japan during his trip.

       2. Another aspect of the problem is the "Buy American" campaign.

          a. Monsanto promises to pay $1000 to any worker who buys a car made in North America.

          b. Even though their bid was lowest, the Los Angeles Transportation Commission canceled a contract with Japan's Sumitomo Corporation to build rail cars.

          c. Jim Reynolds, President of Reynolds Water Conditioning Company, canceled an order for a Nissan car and sold his Infiniti, replacing them with a Ford Escort and a Lincoln Mark VII.

       3. In addition, there is bashing shown in the media.

          a. News broadcasts have shown auto workers bashing Japanese cars with sledgehammers.

          b. We've also seen scenes of car lots with Japanese cars pushed to the back of the lot.

          c. Recent car commercials have made a big deal about Japanese political comments that were taken out of context.

B.   Although, on the surface, the bashing seems to reinforce American patriotism, there are repercussions to it.

    1.   It affects the Pacific Northwest region, which has close trade relations to Asia.

        a.   Japan reaction to protectionist measures could cripple the wheat and lumber industries.

        b.   Boeing would lose thousands of jobs if Japan canceled purchase contracts.

        c.   Japanese businesspeople living in Seattle have made a deal with Seattle politicians to keep the Mariners in the city; this might fall through.

    2.   Protectionist limitations on imports will not solve the problems.

        a.   They cause price increases that we as consumers will have to pay.

        b.   Competition with Japan causes American companies to confront and change their areas of weakness, such as poor workmanship.

    3.   The American economy would suffer.

        a.   Japanese companies employ about 600,000 people in the United States.

        b.   Japanese investors lent us $180 billion, something no other country is willing to do.

    4.   Anger against Japan also affects Asian Americans.

        a.   An American businesswoman of Japanese descent said that businesses had canceled contracts with her, saying, "We don't want to deal with your kind."

        b.   An American of Chinese descent said that strangers approached him, cursed him, and told him to go back to Japan.

        c.   In 1983, a Chinese American was killed by two laid-off auto workers who made "obscene remarks about Asians and Japanese cars" (Zia, 1991, p. 25).

III.   *Conclusion*

A.   We have looked at an important issue facing America today—that of Japan bashing.

B.   As the panelists on the Oprah Winfrey show illustrated, there is a problem that affects our society both economically and racially.

C.   So the next time you are urged to "Buy American," remember that the issue is not as simple as it may seem on the surface.

Adapted from an outline by Victoria Li (1992, April 1). St. John's University.

SAMPLE OUTLINE:
Speech to Persuade (to Actuate)

Topic: Televison Violence
General Purpose: To persuade
Specific Purpose: To persuade my audience to support legislation to protect children from television violence
Central Idea: The increasing number of violent television programs, including cartoons, is potentially harmful to youngsters; we can do something to help solve the problem.

Organizational Pattern: Problem–Solution

I. *Introduction*

 A. We all grew up watching Bugs Bunny, that crazy rabbit who was continually sliced, diced, mashed, or melted and still emerged alive.

 B. Bugs is still around, but he has been joined by other cartoons that have many people concerned about the effects of violence on American children.

   1. Television is many children's closest companion; the average child watches about 5,000 hours of TV by the first grade and 19,000 hours by graduation.

   2. Many parents and psychologists worry that this viewing will have negative effects.

     a. This is more time than they spend in class.

     b. The National Coalition on Violence estimates that an average eighteen-year-old has seen 200,000 violent acts on television.

   3. Others believe TV is not harmful to children, but more than 1,000 scientific studies have shown that this is not true.

 C. I became interested in this topic when I heard about an Ohio child who set fire to his home, killing his baby sister, when he got the idea from MTV's Beavis and Butthead.

 D. Today, I'll persuade you that many television shows are harmful to children, and I will tell you what you can do to be part of the solution.

II. *Body*

 A. There is a problem of TV violence.

   1. One related factor is publicity for various shows.

     a. Each network publicizes its programs through radio, TV, and newspapers.

b. Products such as T-shirts and lunchboxes also publicize the characters.

2. Often preadolescent children do not have the capacity to separate fiction from reality.

a. The Ohio boy who set the fire was one of these.

b. One Indiana school board had to announce that there was no such thing as Mutant Ninja Turtles; children had been crawling down storm drains to find them.

3. Children are born with an instinctive desire to imitate, but they do not yet have an instinct for determining whether a behavior ought to be imitated.

a. The National Commission on the Causes and Prevention of Violence reported that exposure to TV increases the rates of physical aggression.

b. Television networks did their own research to see if this claim was valid; ABC commissioned researchers from Temple University to study young males imprisoned for violent crimes (ex. homicide, rape, assault).

1) In two surveys, 22 percent and 34 percent reported they consciously imitated TV crime techniques.

2) Fortunately, most were unsuccessful!

4. Similar studies show that TV can be harmful.

a. One was conducted by Pennsylvania State University academics.

1) One group of four-year-olds saw a half-hour superhero cartoon three times a week for four weeks.

2) Two other groups saw bland programs.

3) The children who saw the violent cartoons were more likely to hit, shoot, and throw things, according to psychologist Aletha Huston, co-author of the study.

b. In another study, preschoolers who watched a violent superhero cartoon for one month exhibited more aggressive play than a group shown episodes of Mister Rogers.

5. This does not mean that every child who watches violent television programs becomes violent, but it is a factor that affects some people negatively in a culture that has too many acts of violence.

TRANSITION: As you can see, there is a problem with TV violence, and something needs to be done to improve the situation.

    B. Various solutions or remedies have been proposed.

        1. First, and most logical, is that parents or guardians be aware of what children watch and control it.

        2. U.S. Senator Dave Durenberger introduced a bill in the Senate.

           a. It is called the Children's Television Violence Protection Act of 1993.

           b. This bill would require TV shows incorporating violent material to carry parental warnings.

        3. Representative Edward Markey, Democrat from Massachusetts, proposes another bill.

           a. This law would require all sets to contain a V-chip, a microchip allowing parents to block out specific programs when children are left unsupervised.

           b. This bill is still being considered.

        4. Here is how you can act.

           a. Write your congressional representative and support the V-chip legislation.

           b. Or call the congressional switchboard at (202) 334-2121.

           c. If you view a program you feel is too violent, don't be afraid to contact the TV network to express your opinion.

           d. When you watch television with a young child, limit the amount of violence.

III. *Conclusion*

    A. Every Saturday morning and on ordinary weeknights, millions of children glue themselves to the TV set.

    B. The images and shows they watch help shape who they are, and many studies reveal that a number are increasingly violent after watching violence.

    C. It is important that we support legislation such as the V-chip bill in order to protect children from violence on television; again, the congressional switchboard number is (202) 334-2121.

    D. Finally, limit the amount of violence that children see when they are with you, and let your opinions be known to the TV networks.

References

Allman, W. F., & Rainie, H. (1993, July 12). Warning shots at TV. *US News and World Report,* pp. 48–50.

Silver, M. (1993, September 20). Sex, violence, and the tube. *US News and World Report,* pp. 76–78.

Zuckerman, M. R. (1993, August 2). The victims of TV violence. *US News and World Report*, p. 64.

Durenberger, D. (1993, May 31). Monday memo—Editorial. *Broadcasting and Cable*, p. 7.

Kiernan, V. (1993, August 14). A chip to veto violence on television. *New Scientist*, p. 5.

Scharper, S. P. (1990, September 7). Wacky violence in "toons" viewed with fascinated uncritical glee. *National Catholic Reporter*, p. 13.

Centerwall, B. S. (1993, Spring). Television and violent crimes. *Public Interest*, pp. 56–71.

Outline by Kaliopi Petris (1993, December 3). St. John's University. (Adapted)

EVALUATION FORM

Speech to Persuade (General Form)

Name_____ Time _____

Claim:_____

Invention and Disposition

_____Topic appropriate to audience and time
_____Speech purpose clear

Introduction

_____ Attention gained
_____ Related to audience
_____ Credibility revealed
_____ Preview

Body

_____ Clearly organized points
_____ Proofs
_____ Pathos: audience appeals
_____ Ethos: speaker credibility
_____ Rational proofs
_____ Supporting evidence
_____ Adequacy of data/claims/warrants
_____ Evidence of research (sources)
_____ Ethics of argument
_____Transition statements

Conclusion

_____ Signal of end

_____ Review of main points

_____ Tie to introduction

_____ Impact ending/call to action

Style

_____ Language appropriate

_____Vivid language

_____ Clarity

Delivery

_____ Vocal: rate, volume, variation, quality

_____ Pronunciation

_____ Kinesics: posture, gestures, eye contact

_____ Other nonverbals: appearance, space, time

Memory

_____ Fluency of thought

_____ Minimal use of notes

Grade _____

EVALUATION FORM

Monroe's Motivated Sequence

Name_____ Time _____

Claim: _____

Invention and Disposition

I.   Attention step (introduction)
  _____Attention
  _____Related to audience
  _____Credibility established
  _____Previewed

II. Need step
  _____Problem demonstrated
  _____Ramifications given
  _____Use of sufficient support
  _____Pointing to audience need

III. Satisfaction step
  _____Solution described
  _____Solution explained
  _____Need and solution logically connected
  _____Practicality of solution
  _____Objections met

IV. Visualization step
  _____Hypothetical positive results
  _____Hypothetical negatives if not implemented
  _____Contrast

V.   Action step
  _____Summarized
  _____Called for response
  _____Stated personal intention
  _____Ended with impact

Style

_____Vivid language

_____Clarity

Delivery/Memory

_____Vocal: rate, volume, tone, quality

_____Kinesics: posture, gestures

_____Other nonverbal: appearance, space, time

_____Minimal use of notes

_____Eye contact

Grade_____

17

Public Speaking in Organizations

SPEECH ASSIGNMENT:
Group Presentation

Time: 20–25 minutes total

Definition

You will work with a group to discuss a controversial or problematic topic in depth. This list suggests some topics/problems in the news in the last few years.

Skills

All of the abilities of invention, disposition, style, and delivery from previous speeches

Ability to cooperate with a group to discuss a problem in depth

Ability to choose a format that most effectively presents the group's findings to the class

Guidelines

1. Choose a topic that is of interest to you and represents a problem on the campus, local, national, or international level.

2. Meet with a group that shares your interest in the topic and divide up areas of the topic to research individually.

3. Gather information about your topic, using the worksheets that follow.

4. Discuss your information with other members of your group.

5. Decide on a format to present your information. You may want to discuss the issue in a panel format. Alternatively, you may choose to have each group member present only a portion of the material, using the symposium format.

6. If you choose a panel format, decide on the questions your group will discuss. If you use the symposium format, outline your speech.

7. Select one person to introduce the topic and the members of the group; select another to conclude the presentation and open the discussion to the audience.

EXAMPLES

Four students were interested in the *Repressed Memory Syndrome*, the theory that many adult problems are the result of repressed childhood memories—especially those relating to sexual abuse.

Speaker 1 defined repressed memories.

Speaker 2 gave arguments for them.

Speaker 3 gave arguments against them.

Speaker 4 discussed the implications of lawsuits based on them.

A group of students discussed the problem of *campus parking*. They followed the problem-solving method shown in the textbook, pages 416–417. In a panel format, they:

defined the problem

analyzed related facts, causes, effects, values, and policies

discussed criteria for a solution

listed possible solutions

argued for construction of a new parking garage as the best possible solution

A group discussed *immigration issues*. In a symposium format:

One gave the history of immigration, including global immigration.

Another (a student from Vietnam) discussed political asylum.

A third argued that immigrants made the country greater.

A fourth presented the cost of immigration to taxpayers.

Other topics that make good group discussion subjects are:

media violence

grade inflation

male–female differences

home schooling

alternative medicine

the "three strikes and you're out" policy

WORKSHEET:
Research Questions

    A. Questions of fact

        1.

        2.

        3.

        4.

    B. Questions of value

        1.

        2.

        3.

    C. Questions of policy

        1.

        2.

        3.

        4.

WORKSHEET:
Research Citation Form

Magazine:
>   Author
>   Date
>   Title of article
>   Magazine title, volume, page #

_____

_____

Newspaper:
>   Author
>   Title
>   Newspaper
>   Edition
>   page #

_____

_____

Book:
>   Author(s)
>   Date
>   Title
>   City of publication
>   Publishing company

_____

_____

Interview:
>   Person interviewed
>   Place
>   Date

_____

_____

Additional references in similar bibliographic form

_____

_____

EVALUATION FORM

Group Speech

Name_____

Group Topic_____

Group as a Whole

____ Introduction/orientation to topic
____ Purpose of presentation clear
____ Evidence of group co-creation of meaning
____ Transitions
____ Conclusion
____ Question-and-answer period

Group grade ____

Individual Participation

____ Main points clear
____ Variety of support
____ Adequate support
____ Claims warranted
____ Interesting (relevant)
____ Grammar, etc.
____ Evidence of research
____ Sources cited
____ Extemporaneous delivery
____ Conversational
____ Eye contact
____ Vocals

Individual grade ____